Enterprise Risk
Management in a Nutshell

Enterprise Risk Management in a Nutshell

Dennis Cox

 BUSINESS EXPERT PRESS

Enterprise Risk Management in a Nutshell
Copyright © Business Expert Press, LLC, 2017

First published in 2017 by
Business Expert Press, LLC
222 East 46th Street, New York, NY 10017
www.businessexpertpress.com

ISBN-13: 978-1-94709-844-2 (paperback)
ISBN-13: 978-1-94709-845-9 (e-book)

Business Expert Press Finance and Financial Management Collection

Collection ISSN: 2331-0049 (print)
Collection ISSN: 2331-0057 (electronic)

Cover and interior design by S4Carlisle Publishing Services Private Ltd., Chennai, India

First edition: 2017

10 9 8 7 6 5 4 3 2 1

Printed in the United States of America.

Abstract

Risk management is an often used phrase that is rarely fully embedded within the business process and procedures of firms. This text looks at the challenges faced in implementing a risk management framework as well as the key elements of such a framework. It is designed for the business professional that is not an expert in risk management and addresses all of the major risks that are likely to be faced in practice, considering the risk mitigation and measurement techniques that are most likely to be relevant. This is an intermediate text and accordingly does not focus on the mathematical elements but rather provides a readable entry text for anyone seeking information on this important subject.

Keywords

Control, Credit risk, Enterprise risk, Liquidity risk, Operational risk, Risk appetite, Risk framework, Risk management, Risk mitigation

Contents

Background

The purpose of the In a Nutshell series is to fulfil a gap in the market for technical publications. At present, the market has two types of books—those that try to tell you everything and others that try to tell you nothing. The first type of text is typified by a writer who is attempting to show the reader how clever they are by including a level of technical detail that can only be understood by really technical people, such as the writer. The others try to dumb down the material to such a level that it actually provides nothing to anyone.

Well, this is not going to be a technical book. It will seek to avoid unnecessary jargon while explaining why enterprise risk management is more than just a good idea; why, in fact, it makes sense for all firms. However, the book will stop short of telling you everything. That is for other books in this series.

Essentially, this is the first part of a series of books that will look at a variety of areas of business and risk, trying to provide you with the information that you require for your day-to-day purposes, to become familiar without having to become an expert.

Future books will look at a variety of other specialist subjects and will seek to explain the key issues and challenges without losing the reader in mathematical notation or spurious concepts that even the experts know are not really required.

CHAPTER 1

What Is Risk?

In business, everything you do is related to a consideration of risk and reward. Businesses take risks all the time. Risk is not a four-letter word and is not to be avoided. Rather, it is to be managed and controlled. Businesses need to take the risk that it is appropriate for them to take while, at the same time, measuring and managing that risk to ensure that it is effectively aligned with stakeholder expectations.

Let us consider what that is likely to mean in practice. Any business intends to deliver something to someone. Whatever they deliver needs to be of some perceived benefit to the recipient or they would not purchase the goods or service. They could just copy what is on the market already, but there is a risk that the existing product already has an established brand and customer loyalty, forcing the new market entrant to what might be a lower price strategy. They could produce a cheaper version, but it could be less reliable, damaging the new entrant brand. They could try to make the product better than the current market product, but this could involve excessive costs, and the market may not perceive value in the improvement. They could just copy the cost structure and product of the incumbent firms, but this may result in an infringement of patents or copyright.

Every option includes some level of risk, which the firm needs to take to achieve a reward. So, risk is everywhere and needs to be considered appropriately.

By saying that risk is not a four-letter word, I am suggesting that risk should not always be avoided. If a firm takes no risk at all then it cannot do any business, have any staff, or premises, or any customers. It is not possible for a business to operate without taking risks.

All of you reading this book will have taken some risk today, risks that are acceptable to you. You will have woken up. I can be sure of that because sleeping people do not tend to read many books! Having woken up, your first decision of the day is whether or not to get up. You could read the book in bed or read it somewhere else. That is a decision, but what are the risks? If you read this book in bed as soon as you wake up, apart from being a rather sad individual, you will also not have had any breakfast. If you get up and have breakfast, then you may not read the book.

Life is full of decisions and each of these has a risk assessment that needs to be taken into account. To do this, you use the world's greatest neural modeler, which is sitting between your ears.

How does this play out in business? If you decide you want to start a business, you are immediately confronted by a range of questions.

Even the initial question is fraught with risk. Leaving a full-time employed role to start your own business is clearly a risk. However, if you did not have a job, then starting your own business could be seen to be less of a risk. In the first case, the entrepreneur gives up certainty of income and the support of an existing company for the hope of a more successful future. So, what are the risks? They are many, including the following:

- The risk that the new venture will be unsuccessful and will fail because the idea or its implementation are poor
- The risk that the new venture will not be able to raise the funds it needs to meet its liquidity or capital needs
- The risk that the new venture will not have the skills necessary to be successful
- The risk that the entrepreneur will not be able to get a role of equal level once the new venture has failed
- The risk that the partner of the entrepreneur may not share this risk-taking spirit and prefers food on the table and shiny red bicycles for the children, rather than hoping for a future nirvana

So, poverty, loss of status, divorce, and depression are all risks that the entrepreneur needs to face. Of course, the entrepreneur who starts without a job is also taking risks, although some of these may be seen as being lower than that of the successful employee. In this, the final two risks still exist although they could potentially be a little lower. How could you get a lower salary if you do not have a job? Would you be as worried about your future if you were unemployed and did not appear to have much of a future? Without answering any of these issues, it is clear that unemployment and career change can be the catalysts for someone deciding to become an entrepreneur.

Having achieved that transition, I know this to be true.

So, everything in business focuses on the taking and managing of risk. Indeed, I view risk as being the currency of human activity, not money. Making money is often a consequence of risk-taking, not its cause. A gambler putting $400 on 15 at a casino is not doing it with the expectation that they will generally win. There is the balance of hope over experience and money is how the risk is expressed. The risk is better shown through using probability, the probability that the next number will be 15. The gambler knows it probably will not be, but that the return will be great if it is. This return is not only expressed in pure monetary terms, but also in the feeling of wellbeing and elation that the gambler feels. It therefore is not to be measured purely in terms of monetary value. So, risk is a concept that encompasses many things and it is only through obtaining a thorough understanding as to how risk impacts on your business that you will get to the heart of effective enterprise risk management. Indeed, the failure of many firms to fully understand their risk profile and the uncertainties that are inherent in their business is why so many companies fail in practice.

CHAPTER 2

The Role of Enterprise Risk Management

Enterprise risk management has, at its core, a simple concept, that is, that a business needs to at least understand all the risks that it is currently facing or is likely to face in the future. Some of these risks, it will be able to measure and manage; whereas others it will need to react to. Let us start with what is perhaps the normal summary of risks and consider how this leads to enterprise risk management. Generally, risks may be analyzed into the following categories:

- Credit risk
- Market risk
- Liquidity risk
- Operational risk
- Strategic risk
- Reputational risk

As soon as you start with any such analysis, you need to ensure that all of the risks that your firm faces are analyzed and classified under these risk headings. Of course, these risks are all different and they could consequently be measured and managed differently. However, there is a problem with managing risks in silos and this results from the different ways in which they are managed. One of the challenges of effective risk management is to ensure that all risks are managed on a consistent basis enabling management to understand the nature of their risk environment in total.

There is also a concern that there could be a disconnect between the risk function and the management of the enterprise. It is incumbent upon risk professionals to provide their reporting and information in a format and with explanations that are intelligible by their audience and not by other risk professionals.

Returning to the risk analysis, let us consider each of these risks individually. You will then see the issue regarding modelling and data consistency.

Credit Risk

Credit risk is the risk that someone is not going to fully meet their financial or debt obligations. The firm may have sold goods or services to someone. There is then a risk that they will not make the payment in accordance with your payment terms. Credit risk is not just that they may not pay, it is also that they may pay late. If you lend money to a friend, you know you are unlikely to get it back. Again, that is credit risk except that the accounting in this case is debit cash, credit experience.

For credit risk to occur, you will need to be owed something; which, of course, does not need to be cash. If you are building a machine for a customer you may not be able to raise an invoice until the equipment is completed. However, the knowledge that you intend to sell the equipment to a customer means that you are already incurring credit risk even though the invoicing date has not been reached.

If you lend your car to a friend and they do not return it, then this again is probably credit risk. You have lost the monetary value of the car and this is still held by the former friend. In this case, the accounting treatment is debit cash, credit stupidity.

In terms of measuring credit risk, you need to know what you are owed, and this will typically need to be measured in monetary form. By looking at what has happened before, as shown in historic databases, perhaps supplemented by external information which could include agency data, the company is able to assess the likelihood that the customer will meet their obligations. This likelihood is passed on to the clients typically by providing a lower price or discount to the better credit quality customer, and this is what is referred to as differential pricing.

Essentially, credit risk management uses historic data to try to predict the future. That of course leads to the conclusion that credit modelling is at its best when future performance is clearly related to historical loss experience, a theme we will return to later in later chapters.

Market Risk

Market risk arises typically from a change in the price of something. It is not about a change to the market itself since that is actually included within strategic risk, as we shall see later. So, where does market risk tend to turn up? If a company has a commodity that forms part of their product, copper wire for example, or oil, then they will need to acquire the copper or oil before they make their product. The price they will have to pay will fluctuate, based upon the market movements. In the case of commodities there are markets on which these assets are quoted, which can provide a base price, the London Metals Exchange (LME) and the International Petroleum Exchange (IPE), for example.

By looking at movements in price of the specific commodity on the relevant exchange, the firm can see whether the cost of their commodity is rising or falling. The impact of reprising the commodity to market price is market risk, as indeed is the impact of any future change in the price.

Another place where this turns up is in the area of currency risk. Currencies vary considerably, as anyone going on holiday away from their own currency zone knows only too well. If a firm is in the U.S. dollar zone, that is they report in U.S. dollars and the majority of their costs and income is in dollars, then anything they do in a currency other than U.S. dollars is a foreign currency transaction.

If the U.S.-based firm is selling to Germany, they will perhaps have been required to quote their price in Euros. As the rate of exchange between the U.S. Dollar and the Euro varies, the firm will either receive more or less U.S. dollars as a consequence of currency movements. This loss is also market risk. To illustrate this risk, consider the following:

A U.S. company sells industrial equipment to a German company for €125 million. If there is Euro–Dollar parity (in other words $1 = €1), then the U.S. firm will receive $125 million, which is perhaps what they budgeted for. However, if the exchange rate changes to €1.25 = $1, then they will receive only $100 million, a market risk loss of $25 million or a margin loss of 20%.

So just as failing to receive the €125 million payment from the German company would be credit risk, an adverse movement in the Euro/dollar exchange rate would be market risk.

In terms of judging market risk, the required information is generally available on exchanges and markets, with it then being published in public information sources. There is no shortage of information about the past again the past is often used to predict the future. However, this is also supplemented by information about future expectations as shown in forward prices and contracts.

Another area where market risk arises is in equities and bonds. Equities are shares in the ownership of a company normally traded on an exchange. Bonds are essentially loans or debts issued by a firm, which can be traded on a secondary market. Both of these instruments trade on exchanges such as the New York Stock Exchange (NYSE). The NYSE will show the trading price of the instrument in real time, so finding a current market value is not a problem.

Firms hold equities and bonds in two main places. They can hold them directly in their balance sheets or in their pension funds. You could mark these positions to market by working out how much you would actually receive for the position held today by revaluing using the current price on the exchange. The price will have either gone up or down, or stayed the same. Any difference that arises is the consequence of market risk. It is an important concept to understand that market risk is not always negative and that you can be paid for the risks that you are taking, even in an investment environment.

Liquidity Risk

Liquidity risk is another main risk category and is distinct from market risk. Whereas market risk is essentially looking at the impact of an asset or liability being reprised, liquidity risk is dealing with a much simpler concept, that of running out of money.

We all know what running out of money means. You have gone out for an evening with a certain amount of folding currency and some credit cards. Suddenly, you find that you have used all of your currency and your credit cards are being rejected. You have become illiquid.

In companies, this can happen in many ways and some of these are a little counterintuitive. Companies are funded in many different ways, including by the following:

* Equity issuance
* Bond issuance
* Not distributing reserves
* Loans
* Overdrafts
* Credit cards
* Creditors

Any excess assets that the firm holds will be held in some form of investment or cash account.

If the firm is unable to pay its debts, then at some stage, it will have difficulties. It could potentially delay paying creditors or raise more funds from investors or its bank. If it is not able to do any of this it may have a real problem, but there may be other things they can do. It could be that they own a property and can sell this to an investor, leasing it back. The accounts receivable book could also be used to support funding through using either invoice discounting or factoring.

Cash is king in any business and its close management is always important. However, the growing business also requires support. As it grows it takes on more inventory or stock and has increasing debtors or accounts receivable, as well as creditors and accounts payable. Smaller firms are generally paid later by larger firms, which exacerbates the problems for the developing business since it needs to ensure that its staff and suppliers are paid on a timely basis.

The consequence of this is that it is the growing firm that often runs out of cash, rather than the failing firm, which perhaps bizarrely releases cash as it fails. As the firm declines, it uses up its inventory, which it does not replace. Its accounts receivables slowly do pay, but they are also not replaced. At the same time, it does not take on new accounts payable since it will not need new inventory. It is when things turn for the better that the firm tends to have liquidity problems.

How do firms manage liquidity? Market risk looks at the current asset prices and takes that price supplemented by future data if that is available. Credit risk looks at historic information supplemented by external data. This is not really available for liquidity risk.

To understand the liquidity that the firm is likely to need, it will need to understand the business that it is running and how it will change. It needs to know its costs and income in detail. Contractual data is not very helpful since we know that customers often do not pay on time. It is what will actually happen in terms of real cash movements that counts and this is what is referred to as behavioral analysis. What is the actual supplier, customer and cost behavior likely to be?

There is also one other form of liquidity risk to consider. Firms often keep a stock of what are referred to as liquid assets to deal with an emergency of some kind. Smaller firms tend to keep this in cash, held by a bank which it hopes will stay solvent. Other firms will hold a variety of financial instruments, including bonds and equities. The key issue here is to ensure that the asset would be liquid in the environment that is being considered. Greek banks historically have tended to hold Greek government bonds as their prime source of liquid assets. During the Greek banking crisis, when Greek bonds became illiquid, holding them for liquidity purposes was clearly ineffective.

So, there is a lot of thinking to be done in terms of liquidity risk, both in understanding the cashflows within your business and in thinking through what assets are likely to be liquid in the future?

Operational Risk

In the last few years, there has been a lot written about operational risk, which perhaps might make you think that it is a new type of risk. It is not. It is as old as time itself. Operational risk is primarily taken as a consequence of the activity that a firm is conducting. You do not go out to take operational risk, you just get it. When a caveman designed a spear, they attached a flint to a stake to throw at their prey. The binding of the flint to the spear is perhaps the key operation in this process. If the binding were to fail, then no spear, no dinner, and no caveman!

Operational risk looks at everything that we do and considers how much could go wrong. Inherent risk is the risk of everything going wrong without any controls. Effective implementation of controls can clearly mitigate operational risk and losses are evidence of residual risk. So:

$$\text{inherent risk} - \text{controls} = \text{residual risk}$$

The problem is how to manage operational risk. Too many firms have operational risk paranoia and implement controls that lose them value. If in a year you have a loss of U.S.$2,500, but to prevent the loss recurring would cost you U.S.$50,000, then clearly you should take the loss. Essentially, controls are losses that recur every year in the hope that they may mitigate an event that occurs; which they frequently do not.

We design businesses where people are careless and controls help them remain careless. Nobody goes to work with the intention of making a mistake. Nobody says I will make one mistake at 10:15 a.m., another just after lunch at 2:10 p.m., and one just before I leave in the evening at 4:55 p.m. Nobody works like that, but we have firms that are designed to be like that. If nobody ever made a mistake, you would never need a control. Controls are for bad people. If you purely implemented a career development policy of exiting failing staff, then you would find that they might be more careful.

So, we can measure residual risk from loss records except not every operational loss has the word loss in front of it in your records. How do you record an overrun on a computer system or excessive overtime, for example? They are both costs that should not have been incurred, yet they are only shown in accounting records as costs, not losses.

But the greater problem here is in measuring the loss you would make without a control being in place, the inherent loss. If you take away the control, then you will have the loss that you were trying to prevent, which does not sound like a great idea. Think about business continuity planning. You are worried about the loss of your building so you design a business continuity plan, but could you test it? Clearly what you could do is secretly design an explosion at your office at, say, Tuesday at 3:30 p.m. All of your staff that should be there will be there, and of course they will all be killed, which is suppose is just collateral damage. You will then be able to work out exactly what the loss would be, but only there was someone left to do the calculation. If you do choose to adopt this approach, I would recommend that you contact the local press first to let them know that the explosion is not a terrorist event, just your firm testing its plans again!

Instead we use scenario planning and control and risk self-assessment to try to imagine what the loss would be, but we do not really know. Poor loss data. Poor estimation of potential losses. Poorly costed controls. Poorly managed risk.

That leaves us with two main categories of risk to consider, which are also often poorly managed—strategic risk and reputational risk.

Strategic Risk

Does your firm even have a strategy? Who is responsible for it? Does your Board (if you have one) really spend time thinking of strategy or are they really just doing the day-to-day, what might be referred to as tactics?

Strategic risk is the risk that the firm adopts the wrong strategy, which includes the risk of not doing something as much as of doing something. A lethargy strategy is watching everything change around you and failing to grab the opportunity that may then be grabbed either by a new market entrant or a competitor.

Businesses such as Blockbuster Video had a great business and brand based upon renting out videos, but failed to see the change coming in the market that was driven by the emergence of the internet and the availability of downloading of music. Banks (remember them?) failed to see the growth of nonbanks and peer-to-peer lenders.

Since not having the wrong strategy is such an important issue for a firm, it is perhaps surprising that it is often dealt with so poorly. Strategy is a skill that is not within the training of most business managers, so unsurprisingly, they make a bit of a mess of it. Too often we promote people to the level of their incompetence, but that is another story.

Strategic risk is hard to evaluate with any degree of accuracy. Out of all the strategies available to you, why did you select this one? How wrong might you be? The paucity of data and the difficulty of assessing these impacts is perhaps one of the reasons why strategic risk is rarely evaluated effectively.

That just leaves us with reputational risk to consider.

Reputational Risk

What is a business? It is essentially a series of processes and activities that a firm chooses to undertake to meet its strategy (if it has one). Most of these could be copied by another competitor firm without too much trouble. If you consider a services firm such as a law firm or accountancy firm, what are they? What makes them special? Do they do anything that their competitors do not do or could not copy? What then makes you pay more or prefer one firm over another? The key elements of the value of the firm are:

- The brand
- Any trademarks
- The customers
- Any intellectual property
- The staff

What these have in common is that none of these appear in the accounts. That an accountancy firm is a brand just as Coca Cola is a brand might be depressing for the accountants, but is a fact of life. What this means is that a reputation that has taken years to build can be shredded in a few days; just remember Arthur Andersen, for example.

If reputation is key, then reputation needs to be protected. Banks used to have strong reputations; now they are less popular than traffic wardens. I used to be proud to say I worked in the banking industry. Now I would rather say I worked as an undertaker. At least nobody is then likely to ask me any more questions, and of course, I could not take my work home with me. Problem with repeat business though . . . .

Who in your firm is responsible for its reputation and what do you do to protect it? How do you manage it or how could you improve it? Reputational risk is easy to measure by using a simple metric, as follows:

1. An event must happen (although it does not need to be under your responsibility).
2. It must become public.
3. And the public must care.

Clearly, the first time someone gets something wrong, there is one level of loss, but if it then repeats, it is much worse. When BP used the Gulf of Mexico as an oil storage facility, this was a disaster both ecologically and in terms of reputation. Were this to recur for BP, this could critically damage their reputation whereas if it happens to one of their competitors then their brand would probably improve.

CHAPTER 3

The Key Building Blocks

Enterprise risk management has a clear series of objectives attempting to ensure that the business both knows and can consider the risks that it is facing and those that it might face. Quantification is important to enable progress, in terms of reducing the level of risk faced, to be clearly monitored by and reported to senior management.

There are a series of key building blocks that are included in all risk programs frameworks. These include the following:

- Senior management support
- Risk appetite
- Risk identification
- The risk register
- Control and risk self-assessment
- Key risk indicators
- Risk consistency
- Stress testing and scenario modelling

There will be other elements that could be included within a risk management framework, but these initial elements should be common to all programs (hopefully).

Senior Management Support

Senior management need to understand the purpose and benefits of the risk management framework. It is not easy being a director of a business in the current world; there are so many things to worry about. With continual changing regulation, employment rules, the changing markets and the global environment being harder to predict, management are so worried about the day-to-day that it can be hard to get them to focus on what might seem to be an arcane requirement. Remember that most senior managers are not actually qualified for the roles that they are fulfilling. Many have no qualifications at all. In a world where bankers, analysts, and other stakeholders are concerned about short-term issues, it is hard to get senior management to focus on what is really important.

Enterprise risk management is important, but it does cost money to implement a proper system. If senior management do not fully appreciate the value of implementing a risk management framework, then they will be unlikely to support it. For the program to be successful, it is necessary to have both their support and their input. If senior management cannot understand why this is being implemented, then they will not be providing the program with the impetus for success that it requires.

Obtaining senior management support is never easy. Boards and senior management teams are made up of individuals with a selection of backgrounds and experience. They bring their prejudices, interests and knowledge to everything that they do. I wish to make one thing crystal clear. As a risk professional without senior management support, you are bound to fail and I will explain this in more detail later.

Engaging with Senior Management

The challenge for the Enterprise Risk Management project leader is to find a way to engage with the senior management team in a way that has resonance to them.

There are a range of approaches that could be adopted, some of which may be appropriate to your firm. However, each comes with a level of associated risk. Taking the wrong approach in the wrong firm could easily become career-limiting!

First piece of advice: A void jargon when communicating with senior management.

One of the problems I have seen is that risk managers are keen to show senior management how clever they are and do so by using technical language that a mere mortal without a couple of math's degrees would never understand. The mistake being made by the risk manager is that management already know you are clever; that is why they have hired you. Showing management that you think they are stupid is not really a good way to progress.

Remember that there are no such things as stupid questions, only stupid answers. Whatever question is being posed is obviously a concern to the person who is asking it. You should answer it as carefully and controlled as you can be.

Second piece of advice: Never underestimate the stupidity of your senior management.

Senior management come in a variety of shapes and sizes and each has its own problems. From my experience, it is not necessarily appropriate to assume that they are either logical or numerate. As a risk manager, there is always a requirement to provide options to senior management so that they look like they are making the decision.

Normally, the choices provided by the Risk Management function will be nirvana, pestilence and plague. The risk team will expect the senior management team too select nirvana, whereas in practice they do tend to select plague or pestilence. You now have a problem. While they have selected what you consider to be the wrong answer, you cannot let them know that you biased the choices. You are stuck with plague or pestilence and when it all goes wrong it could be seen as your fault.

Their lack of numeracy skills is also a concern. Recently when trying to explain why expenses could not reduce by 350 percent, I ended up resorting to using the fruit bowl.

"OK – here is an apple. Let's take away 100 percent of the apples. How many are left?"

"There aren't any left"

"So, where will the other two and half apples come from??"

I am far from certain that they were either convinced or really understood the point.

But risk managers make this even worse. We talk about confidence levels and values as if we know things with a level of accuracy that we know is not viable. Why should your senior management team understand confidence levels? If you are discussing with them a loss of $10 million with a 95 percent confidence level, they will hear that you are saying they will lose $10 million, whereas you are trying to say something quite different. You are trying to say that most of the time they will not lose $10 million, but they could lose more than that amount. Is that so hard to say? At least they would understand you.

Third piece of advice: Do not rely upon regulations as the reason for doing something

If you must fall back on regulation to justify something that you are recommending, then you will never win the argument. You need to find a way to communicate with them in a language they understand that has a resonance with them. As soon as you start to talk about rules and regulations, you can hear the snoring and the rumbling of tummies.

Regulation might be the driver for what you want to achieve. Your challenge is to come up with a reason for doing things that means something for your audience.

Recently, I was trying to explain stress testing to a Board, which included a retired general. I talked about the number of bullets you give a soldier and suggested that you would typically give them 40 percent more than you expected them to use, that being a stress test.

The Chairman of the Board called over and said I had done something that nobody else had achieved — I had managed to wake up the general! By talking about the bullets that you might need, rather than the ones you would definitely need, I had engaged usefully with the Board to enable them to understand why what they were doing was so important.

Final piece of advice: Make them believe they are fully engaged in the process.

The Board does need to give input into the process. They know the strategy of the firm and it is the strategy that drives the risk management program. However, they do not need to know everything that you are developing.

Risk Appetite or Tolerance

Often spoken about, but rarely understood, risk appetite is a key concept and will be discussed in more detail in the next section. As a basic definition, it is the level of divergence from goals and missions that is unacceptable to stakeholders. It is clearly an all-risk figure and indeed, that is where the complexity arises. It is a driver of behavior and a key building block.

Risk Identification and Register

Before any firm can introduce enterprise risk management, they need to first identify the risks that they are facing. To achieve this, they require some form of risk register with clear risk definitions, although creating such a document is no easy task.

This is a business-owned document consolidated and reported to senior management and driving behavior. It is not a regulatory construct; rather it is crucial to the development of a successful enterprise risk management framework. It needs to incorporate both the risks that the firm manages and those that are outside of its direct control. There are actions to be taken and these need to be considered.

Most of your team will not have any understanding of risk, so asking them to populate a database is essentially unrealistic. Accordingly, much work needs to be conducted to enable the exercise of developing the risk register to be successful. Again, we shall return to this subject later.

Control and Risk Self-Assessment

The logic of this part of the framework is that management have the best understanding of their control environment and how this could be improved. Whether this is actually the case, as we shall consider later, the goal of control and risk self-assessment is to obtain the views of management as to how they will improve their control environment, but it does more than this.

Enterprise risk management seeks to achieve an optimum balance of control against risk, which is consistent throughout the business.

Control and risk self-assessment achieves the necessary management buy in as the importance of the process. There are acknowledged problems, but at its most basic through linking risk to control and subsequently monitoring a well-managed program enterprise risk management can add significant value.

Key Risk Indicators

This is another topic that is often referred to, but is poorly understood. In any business, there are a wide range of indicators, many of which are not risk indicators and certainly, are not key risk indicators.

There are essentially three types of indicator to consider:

- Key risk indicators
- Key control indicators
- Key performance indicators

These are all quite different. First, not all indicators are key. Key indicators are of course important, attached to their impact on risk appetite. Many indicators are useful, but not key. What that means in practice is that they will not need to be reported to senior management.

Key control indicators tell you that a key control is operating as expected and identify when problems are being faced. A key control indicator is required where a control materially mitigates risk as measured against risk appetite.

Performance indicators are different since they tell you that an adequate level of performance is being provided. For example, the length of time that it takes to answer the phone is a performance issue. If the phone is not answered, the consequence could be a disgruntled or lost client, so there is a loss. However, whether the performance is adequate is judged against targets and objectives, rather than against risk.

Key risk indicators inform management as to the potential arrival of a material risk. They are always weighted metrics since it is unrealistic to expect a single metric to be effective in identifying future problems. You will know if you have an appropriate suite since the key risk indicator should flash if an event occurs that exceeds the unitary risk appetite.

Risk Consistency

A vision for enterprise risk management is crucial to the development of a successful risk management framework. Clearly, enterprise risk management considers all risks and the correlations between them. There is no point in being able to tell your Board that if an event happens, you will have credit losses at a certain level if you fail to explain the impact on other risk types. For this to be conducted effectively, there is a need for consistency in modelling approaches between risks. Unless the person building the framework has risk consolidation as a primary objective, the work that is conducted will be severely flawed.

Stress Testing and Scenario Modelling

The final key building block is stress testing and scenario modelling. Too many Boards focus on the day-to-day management of the business to the detriment of ensuring operational and future business resilience. Management should be able to protect the business operations as they work on a regular basis, so the Board should not spend their time editing such work. Rather they should focus on the things that might happen and their impact on the strategy and profitability of the firm.

Sensitivity analysis takes one of the key variables of the business and seeks to appreciate the impact of a unitary movement. This might be the impact of a 1 percent increase in raw material prices, for example. If such an event occurs, the firm may be able to increase its prices or improve efficiency such that the full cost of the increase in prices is not faced directly. Sensitivity analysis provides information on the profitability of the business and the importance of key variables.

Stress testing takes this to a plausible extreme. Clearly costs cannot become infinite since nobody has infinite funds; consequently, an infinite increase in prices is not plausible. Basically, it takes expectations to the level where the relationships between variables break down. It enables a trend to be identified and actions to be considered if the plausible event occurs. It is useful for management in trying to think of things that might happen before they actually happen.

Scenario modelling is a different technique. Scenarios do not arise as a consequence of a trend; rather they just occur like fires, earthquakes and terrorist events. Again, their value is in terms of considering the actions that would potentially be available were such an event to occur. Without some form of management action resulting, the process becomes purely a waste of time.

CHAPTER 4

Risk Governance

Risk management needs to be the way that a firm does business. A successful business both takes risk and receives the appropriate reward for the risks that it is taking. You would expect this to be a key concern of the Board, yet in many firms the boards are not really actively engaged in the process.

Risk management looks both at the present and the future. The Board, in considering the strategy and goals of the firm, should do so in the context of risk and reward. They should then build a risk management framework that seeks to minimize the likelihood that the goals and missions will not be met.

This needs the Board to be conversant with the principles and objectives of risk management and for them to be able to synthesize the information provided to them, leading to both challenge and action. This would suggest that there should be non-executive directors with risk expertise to supplement and challenge the skills of the in-house team. However, few boards currently include an independent risk specialist to achieve this.

Ever board meeting should have risk management on its agenda and this should be included in the terms of reference of the Board. All Board members should receive the level of training on risk that is commensurate with their role and enable them to understand the data provided to them. This issue regarding Board training must not be understated. We do see a disconnect between the risk functions in some firms and their Boards. The risk functions assume a level of knowledge and understanding of their Board members, which is quite simply not there. The consequence is that you have the ill-informed preaching to the diverted. Basically, it does not work.

The Board needs to be conversant with the terms and techniques used by the risk function. They do not need to be experts, but they do need to be in a position such that they could ask intelligent questions.

The next issue is the reporting lines within the firm. If you look at a typical business reporting structure, it will have a Board and a remuneration (or nominating) committee together with an audit committee. There is rarely an obligation for a risk committee within the local rules and regulations although it is probably recommended for firms commensurate with their size and level of complexity. In the financial services industry, for example, this is generally a requirement. However, when you look at the structures, you may start to see the problem.

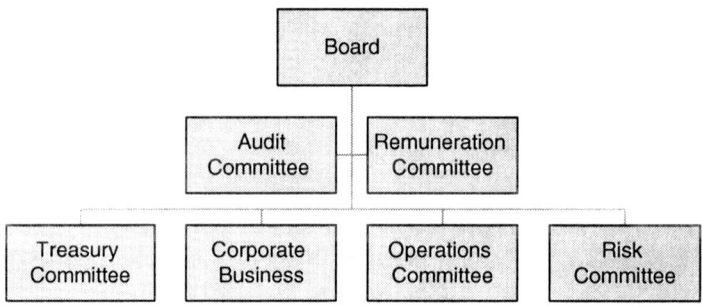

This simple structure clearly leaves out many other potential committees, including human resources and strategy, for example. However, even looking at this simple structure, issues start to be identified and this relates to the scope of each committee as set out in their terms of reference or charter.

Each committee will seek to look at issues that fall within their area of specific responsibility as set out in the terms of reference or charter of the committee. The treasury committee will be looking at the future funding requirements of the firm as well as the day-to-day risk mitigation and cash placement activities that are always required to be undertaken. Two key risks that then influence their work are market risk and liquidity risk. Market risk will result from the positions that the firm is taking in both its investment and its capital portfolios. Any asset that needs to be marked to either market or model can reduce in value, and movements in markets clearly impact this. If this is being discussed at the treasury committee, then the discussion needs to be consistent with the discussions that will take place at the risk committee.

This logically leads into the discussion regarding liquidity risk. Liquidity risk looks at the funding needs of the business now and in the future and seeks to ensure that sufficient liquid assets and facilities are available to meet those obligations. To really understand this, the treasury committee needs to receive reliable behavioral data that properly identified what actually happens within a business, as opposed to what is contractually expected to occur. Contractually, every customer pays on time whereas experience shows that this is rarely the case. Behavioral finance shows what is expected to be the true position in a range of potential scenarios.

Again, if this is being discussed at the treasury committee, how will this feed into the deliberations at the risk committee. Another similar area is what we call counterparty credit risk, which is the risk posed to the firm by other financial institutions. This risk again frequently is discussed within treasury, whereas it is certainly an issue for risk management.

As we mentioned earlier, risk management seeks to look at all the risks that a firm faces to consider risk mitigation strategies that are optimal for the firm as a whole. Separating this between committees can result in actions being taken that might be considered as optimal in the context of the individual committee, but not in the context of the firm as a whole.

The operations committee can also overlap with the risk committee in that operations losses will normally be reported to and investigated by the operations committee. So long as the information is provided in summary form to the risk committee, then this is unlikely to be a significant issue; however, the risk committee is intended to be independent of the daily operations and is therefore better placed to consider the full implication of an issue as opposed to the purely operational issue.

This leads to some form of matrix management structure being applied, perhaps as follows:

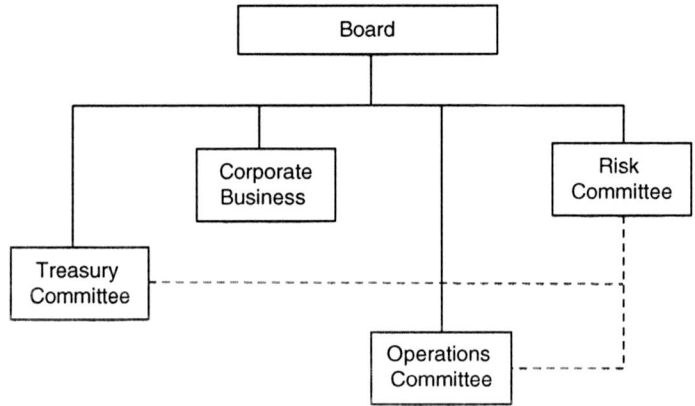

In this structure, there is a matrix reporting line between the treasury committee and the risk committee and also between the operations committee and the risk committee. This has the advantage of enabling each committee to meet the demands of its terms of reference and to report appropriately to the Board, while at the same time providing the risk committee with the information that they need to do their work effectively.

Matrix reporting lines are quite common in business generally and is present in an area such as risk management which, by its nature, is across everything that the firm does.

The next issue to consider is the structure of the risk management function itself. Following on from the risk register creation, the firm will know the risks that it is facing. The question is "What is the best approach to ensure that these are reviewed and managed appropriately at the risk committee?" Of course, there can be no single right answer since the approach adopted will depend on the nature, size and complexity of the firm.

If we consider a major bank, for example, then the following risk categories will probably be suitable:

- Credit Risk
- Market Risk
- Liquidity Risk
- Operational Risk
- Strategic Risk
- Reputational Risk

The question is how these risks would be dealt with and would there be a team within risk management looking at each of these issues. In many firms, there is not a separate strategic risk or reputational risk function within risk management and the market and liquidity risk functions are often merged.

If we look at the following structure:

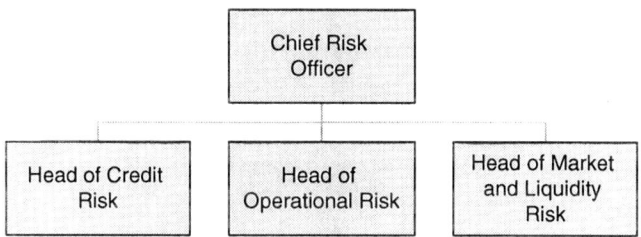

This means that the other risks (strategic and reputational) will only be dealt with at the Chief Risk Officer (or CRO) level. But there are two main other areas that need to be considered: risk models and enterprise risk management. The structure needs to be sufficiently detailed such that it is clear how these risks are dealt with effectively. If there is a separate enterprise risk management function, then it will essentially need to receive reports from all of the parts of risk management. The model risk team will take responsibility for looking at models for every area of risk management and will also have an obligation to ensure that they are consistent. This leads to the following structure:

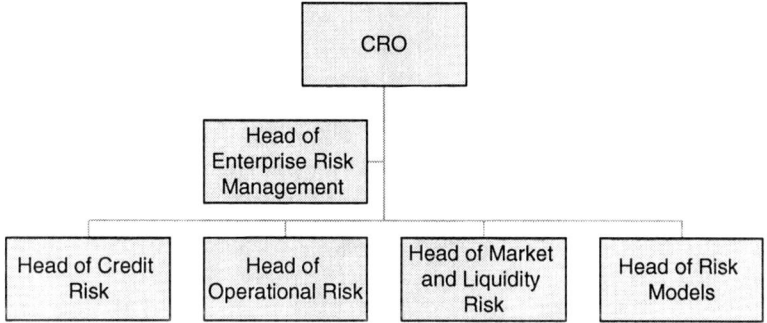

So, a variant of this structure will tend to work well with the Head of Enterprise Risk Management bringing together all of the disparate risk strands together with strategic and reputational risk. Notice that no operational business units have been included within responsibilities of the function. Generally, documentational and administrative business units do not fit well into a risk management function since they essentially drag the CRO into the day-to-day of the business when the role is intended to be forward-looking. Further, at the risk committee meetings, the documentational and administrative units tend to not really feel that they belong. What this often means in practice is that this type of business unit is really badly managed within risk management and is much better placed within the operations area, reporting to the Chief Operating Officer (COO) or the equivalent role.

Of course, this only deals with the structure of the department and how it should report. The problem to consider is how do issues raised within the business get reported quickly and effectively to the risk management function, leading to action. This requires embedding risk management in the business.

Too often, when you start to discuss risk management with the head of a business unit, you receive a response that it is done by the risk management function. The risk management department does not actually do anything since all decisions are really taken by the business itself. This goes to the heart of the three lines of defense model.

CHAPTER 5

Embedding Risk Management in the Business

Put at its most basic, as a business I do not need the greatest risk management function; rather, I need the greatest risk management and that requires risk management to be embedded within the business units themselves (the front line of the business or the first line of defense).

This is an easy thing to say, but a difficult thing to actually achieve. Staff will only understand what the purpose of risk management is if they both see its value and that senior management really believe in it and its importance. Embedding is never easy and many great risk management programs have failed for this simple reason.

If you were appointed risk management of a team that had failed to embed risk management, what would you do? This falls into the challenge equals opportunity debate. It will be a challenge and cannot be achieved quickly. Start with realism. Be realistic in what you can achieve for nothing is going to come easily. Staff will not have any real understanding of risk or the goals and objectives of risk management. They will not have any ability to answer difficult questions on risk assessment or appreciate what they should do with confidence levels. They have been hired to do a job, not to think how they should do their job. Basically, they are not trained to achieve your goals. They are too busy doing what they are paid for.

You will need to demonstrate your worth to the business units and to show that their implementing good risk management techniques is good for the company, and therefore, also good for them. Do not use jargon or rely on regulation, because if you do that, you will have probably already lost the argument. Unless the values in what you are seeking to achieve are obvious to the front-line team, your project is doomed to failure.

So, how can this be done? Slowly and with great care.

You need to spend time with each front-line business, understanding what challenges they really have and what can go wrong. Considering where they can make losses, where they could be more efficient and where they could make more profit. You need to be someone that helps them to solve things and then to introduce tools that assist them to achieve this same aim. Simple solutions are normally the best ones to start with, so that you build the level of trust that is required. None of this is difficult in principle, but too many risk management specialists try to be elitist and to keep what they are doing to themselves. The risk management function does not manage the risk in the business. Instead, this is achieved by the front office teams. These are the people that actually do something.

I always start with the first line of defense, which is the staff that actually make a real difference. The second line of defense are the people that check and monitor the first line of defense. The third line of defense (internal audit) check the first line of defense and whether the second line of defense are checking the first line of defense. Risk management knows what to do with defense. They sit on it.

Risk management is not just a dumping ground for everything that does not belong anywhere else. Their role is to ensure that the business develops systems of control and structures that deliver the goals and missions of the firm in accordance with its risk appetite, of which more later. In working with business units, good risk management behaviors need to be seen to be part of the way that they work. Loss is not in itself a four-letter word. Losses are the consequence of the control function that they have chosen to implement aligned to their risk appetite. This is a decision that is made by senior management implemented within the business.

Losses can be budgeted for and included into product pricing. They can be monitored and managed. The risk management team may well undertake complex calculations for their own use and to support reporting to senior management if senior management can understand what you are doing. However, much of this has little relevance to the front office and they will not react well to it.

You need to get out there and build. Nothing can be achieved from sitting in your office and sending out instructions. Nobody will understand their relevance and they will not take your role seriously.

The front-line staff understand that if they fail to deliver what is expected of them, then this is likely to be career limiting. They know that if there are events that they did not expect, then they will have a problem in trying to get this properly understood without achieving their own dismissal. If risk management can help them to build a system to reduce the likelihood that unexpected things will occur, then this is surely a good thing and something that they will work on. They will understand its value and see you as a partner in helping them to achieve their own objectives.

Always start with the identification process. Remember that risk identification is a combination of bottom-up and top-down work. There are some risks that every business unit clearly has—internal fraud, fire, or loss of key skills, for example. Each risk needs to have a clear definition that will resonate with the individual business unit and be in the language that they will understand, not in the nerd language of a consultant. These are a given and you do not initially need to spend a lot of time on these. Then, there are risks that are directly associated with the business unit, that really matter to the local management. These need to be identified with the greatest of care. Not each of these will actually be a discrete risk; indeed, many of them will be elements of another risk.

In building the risk register for the business unit, the risks need to appear in the language that the unit understands best and this then also needs to be capable of being consolidated into a single model by the risk management function. Accordingly, clarity of purpose is required. If you allow each unit to come up with their own definitions, then you will have no chance of building a consistent structure.

They will have multiple computer systems that they will be working with. Some of these they will immediately recognize as computer systems, such as data entry packages. Others, such as word processing and spreadsheet software, they will not recognize as computer systems. In reality, the main systems used by many firms are spreadsheet software solutions since all management reporting appears to be based on such spreadsheets.

So, the risks need to align to the business unit and ideally the register needs to be complete. It should not just be a list of the risks that the business is controlling, but instead it should also include those that it should control. It does not just include risks that occur all the time, but also those that could occur infrequently or could potentially occur.

When you start with this work, it is always worth spending time with the local management to understand where they have problems and what has previously gone wrong. If you know what has gone wrong in the past, then you know that risks should have been recognized. The management ought to know about these since this will have cost them bonuses or stress.

Teasing out the others is a true skill and means that the facilitating risk specialist needs to spend time understanding the nature of the activity and the problems faced. Some of this required material will appear in monitoring reports from another part of the second line of defense and other material will be in internal audit reports from the third line of defense. Apart from that, the risk specialists will still need to start doing some fundamental research because good risk management is not just about what you see, but what you should see. The local management will only know what they do and what has gone wrong in the past, since this is what they have always done. They are less likely to know what they should be doing and this is another challenge for you.

If you go in having done the right level of research, you will be able to engage with the local management as an equal. Too often risk managers seem to think that every business unit is the same and fail to do their research. This cannot make sense and it essentially insults the front line, doubting their value. It is condescending and a mistake.

Embedding risk management is about building controls and systems into the way things are done that identify problems before they occur and give management time to prevent their occurrence. It is about looking at how automation of process can provide assistance to the management. It is not about blaming people for things; rather it is about working together to improve the way things are done to prevent recurrence of a specific problem. When risk management is working well and is effective, management will perceive problems that could occur before they occur and take action to prevent them.

As limits and controls are slowly implemented by the management team, they could initially think that they are having their time wasted. They may not perceive the value of having these additional controls. And then the time will come when the control will have saved them from a disaster. That is a disaster for them in their terms, for example, of losing their job. Perhaps only then will they will see the value. Sometimes, it is only after disaster strikes that they really grab the importance of the idea.

The reporting from the business unit will then include naturally risk-based reporting. It will be part of the way that they work. The key problem remaining is risk quantification and that is addressed in the next chapter.

CHAPTER 6

The Problem of Quantification

If I ask you what level of fraud could occur in your business, how would you answer? What value would you give me? Have you ever had to deal with a fraud? If you have, is that the value that you would provide? But this is just one occurrence. How would you know what the value of another fraud might be? How could you know how often frauds might take place? You only have a sample of one.

Where risk management often makes a mistake is in asking people questions that they cannot realistically be expected to be able to answer. They have little or no information, limited experience and inadequate training. Of course, all the staff will need to receive some training in risk management. That is a given. However, this high-level training will only enable them to understand some of the tasks that they are being asked to do and why they are important. It will not enable them to come up with the mathematical answer that the risk manager wants. How could it? Every business unit is different.

The embedding of risk management within the business needs to come up with answers that are consistent within individual units and also between businesses. Clearly, that is going to be difficult to achieve.

Risk is always a distribution, a curve; the only problem is we do not know the shape of the distribution. The expected end of the curve we may know something about. That information will come from internal loss data, which again we shall discuss in more detail later. But there are other problems as well. When something goes wrong and a loss is incurred in excess of a budget, this could be because the event was unusual by its nature. It could also be because the event was unusual by its frequency. Finally, it could also be a consequence of the control system that you have implemented.

Put at its simplest, you might expect to have items of inventory that need to be discarded because they are faulty. You might expect to have to discard $10k per year, which might be made up of 200 items. You do not expect to have to dispose of $100k or 20,000 items. You also do not expect to lose all of your inventory. The first is a loss that is unusual by frequency (and consequently, amount) whereas the second is the loss that is unusual by its nature (a fire, for example).

If you have a sprinkler system in your office, you hope that it will work and put out a fire. There is the risk that the sprinkler system will not work or will be inadequate and that you will still lose your building if there is a fire. There is also the risk that there is a failure in the panel leading to the sprinkler system being activated and that you will have your building and staff soaked without fire. This type of loss is a consequence of the implementation of the control or what might be called a second level of risk.

So, taking all of this into account, how could anyone answer a question such as "How much would you lose"? There are lots of answers to the question, starting with what you expect, which is normally a conservative overestimate. Is what you expect in a year? In a week?? The next loss itself???

What risk need to focus on is what they need. If losses are being incurred, then budgeting for them is a good thing as is monitoring them. It allows the business to regularly consider whether the control system they have implemented remains appropriate or whether it should be improved.

It also facilitates including these costs into product pricing since activity-based costing is the best way to know that your sales price covers all of your costs, including where possible, indirect costs. Direct costs are those that relate directly to the item being manufactured, for example, time spent on a lathe milling engineering parts. Indirect costs need to be allocated to the product and include things such as management time and systems support. And risk management.

So, we need to know actual losses and these need to be recorded by the business unit in their language, which the risk management function know how to consolidate with other business units. You might call it a hammer. I might call it a portable percussion persuasion instrument. As long as we both know what we call it and we can easily translate between the two, then this will work.

You can compare the actual losses over a period of time and see how they change. This will start to give you information that is helpful both to the business and to risk management as to how variation actually takes place. However, what this is not going to tell you is what could happen that has never happened before. Good risk management is about trying to see what might happen and to stop it happening. So now you need mystic Meg.

Be very careful with quantification. The business unit management might be in a position to provide you with an estimate of the worst possible loss that could occur. What might happen if one of your competitors stole all your key trained staff? How many losses would you have then? What might you lose?

I would not ask the management how likely this type of event would be since they would have little ability to answer the question. As a risk manager, I might define such an event at a 99.9 percent confidence level. However, when communicating to management I might refer to it as a once-in-a-year event or something similar.

What risk management will be doing is using this estimated data to anchor the tail of their loss distribution. They will then use the actual loss data to populate the expected part of the distribution. Most management do not need to know that there is a distribution. Instead, what they need to focus on is that if the unexpected happened, what would they do to mitigate the loss. Embedding risk management is about action and thinking through options in advance of an event occurring.

I might refer to this unlikely event as being the maximum potential loss or MPL. The internal loss data will always give me the shape of the expected part of my curve and the maximum loss, another point in the tail. It will not tell me much about the shape of the tail, so you will still need to do a lot of thinking with the team understanding and appreciating what could go wrong and the different tail events that could occur. Stick to being in the real world though. There is no point in trying to assess the impact of being invaded by Martians or in working out the loss if everyone is dead. If everyone one is dead, whether you have a plan or not is not a worry. There would be nobody to implement it—including you.

Typically, as discussed, risk management will look at the shape of the expected losses as demonstrated by the internal loss data, and then use that to build a curve anchoring the distribution using the maximum potential loss. There is also no point in doing severity calculations with business units. What are they supposed to do with this information? If you are told that you could lose $10 million with a 1 percent probability, then severity would be calculated as follows:

$$\$10m \times 1/100 = \$100k$$

But I have told you anything about a loss of $100k. I have been considering a $10 million loss that may or may not occur and have said that it probably will not occur most of the time. Indeed, 99 times out of a 100, it will not occur. If the $10 million loss is unacceptable to your management, what you have said is that it could occur, and therefore management need to implement controls and actions to prevent its occurrence.

One potential use of severity is to compare this value to the cost of an additional control. Some risk managers say that if the cost of the additional control needed to prevent the event is less than the severity, then you should implement it, but again, I would reiterate that care needs to be taken. We were not discussing a $100k loss. We were talking about a remote event that could result in a $10 million loss. Sounds to me that we need to move into the area of insurance, options and mitigating actions.

When the risk function reports their information to the business management, they do seem to like to show how clever they are. Their models will show risk data to a number of decimal places. Once in 3,000 years, they might report that you could lose $48.4 million. What does management hear? Once in 3,000 years. 3,000 years ago . . . was that when Stonehenge was built? It was before the Romans. 3,000 years. What they are thinking is that they will be dead anyway, so who cares.

Anyway how accurate could the figure of $48.4 million be? If you would be wiped out at $10 million, then who cares about the $48.4 million loss? Presumably, the figure you are giving is the center of some form of estimate, but there is massive uncertainty. None of us can really know for sure what loss could occur to us. We can find out what losses have occurred to other firms from external loss data and scale it so it can be applied to our firm in some way, but that will never be accurate. We can develop a curve from our expected data and estimate the tail from the shape of the curve, but that also is only an estimate. Most estimates of this type could be easily wrong by 25 percent, so what is the point in saying $48.4 million? You could say you have estimated a loss value off between $36.3 million and $60.5 million, but you might as well have said it was probably between $35 million and $60 million. You do not know much more than that, so what is the point in setting yourself up for failure by including spurious accuracy within your reporting?

CHAPTER 7

Risk Appetite

As we have mentioned, risk appetite is perhaps the most important single concept within enterprise risk management. Yet, it is rarely implemented effectively. There is not even a single agreed definition as to what risk appetite is. What we are all agreed upon is that it is important, whatever it is.

Some people use a definition as to the level of loss that should not happen, but for me, that only deals with part of the story. Clearly, risk appetite must be more than that since, for example, if you miss an opportunity, then you may lose out to a competitor. This clearly would still be unacceptable. So, any definition of risk appetite should be able to deal both with what is normally seen as a loss and also what could result in a loss of profit.

I tend to use the following definition:

The level of divergence from goals and missions that is unacceptable to my Board

In using this definition there remain problems that we need to deal with. The first is that many firms have really poorly drafted and created goals and missions, which cannot easily be turned into something that can be measured. Statements such as "We want to be the largest," "We want to be the prettiest," and similar statements are rarely the actual goal and mission. The goals typically have something to do with the maintenance of brand value and other intangibles that make the company what it is and what it wants to be. Or it is just to make more money.

In terms of the mission, what risk management want is a number. They will then ensure that the business has designed systems and controls to ensure that the level of divergence from goals and missions does not exceed the risk appetite value in any particular year. Again, in my revised definition you will see I have now included a specific reference to the time period I am using for assessment, so perhaps we could extend the definition a bit as follows:

The level of divergence from goals and missions that is unacceptable to my Board in the one-year time horizon

Another question is how will you calculate the risk appetite? Again, there is no single agreed methodology. As I have said, to come up with something that works in practice. I usually need a number, but we do need a basis to calculate it.

What needs to be done is to get senior management to think through what really matters to them and how they would judge success. This is not about public statements of being nice to bunnies and saving the world. Rather, it is about what they really would see as being completely unacceptable.

If you ask management upfront for numbers for this, they will tend to give you numbers that are too low and could result in your over controlling your business. This value could be the losses (or losses of profit) that they would not like, but they are probably not mission critical losses, which is what you are really looking for.

The unacceptable level of loss that we are seeking is the one that might lead to the resignation of the Board of directors or the failure of the firm. The Board of directors should have some idea as to what this could be. It might relate to loss of growth, loss of profit, loss of market share, loss of expectation of future growth, loss of liquidity, loss of re- serves so you cannot pay dividends . . . There is quite a list of possible measures. What the risk management team needs to do is to identify what are the right measures for your firm and then build them into a consistent model.

In practice, I plot each of the identified measures on a simple number line and identify an area where they all overlap. For each measure, I do not just ask the management to come up with a single number, but instead ask them what numbers they think the number sits between. They tend to find this a little easier to think through. So, you end up with something that looks a bit like this:

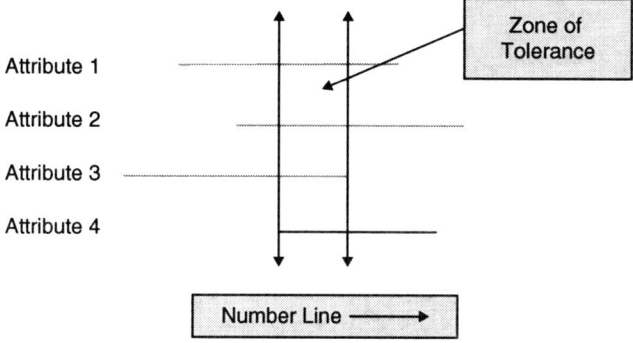

This leads to an area which I refer to as the Zone of Tolerance. Nothing magical here. While I do not know the actual number, I know it sits within the Zone of Tolerance. We do not know what the actual risk appetite value is, but we do know that it sits within the zone of tolerance. Of course, if the metrics do not overlap, you may need to eliminate some metrics that are producing an excessive risk appetite. Basically, the analysis enables you to identify what are the real attributes that help you come up with risk appetite. In the graphic, I have suggested four attributes, which might be loss of market share, loss of growth, loss of profitability, and loss of capital. That would mean that other attributes have been eliminated already.

So, risk appetite starts from the Board, but the risk manager needs to take them on a journey here as well. Actually, most Boards have very little understanding of what is really unacceptable. For my firm, any reduction in turnover is currently unacceptable, as is the loss of liquidity. I cannot afford to make any form of loss since I run a small firm. So, these are probably the metrics I would select.

Now, the risk management team need to do their magic. As we have already discussed, there are a variety of risks that face any business and we collect them in a series of buckets that we call by different things, as follows:

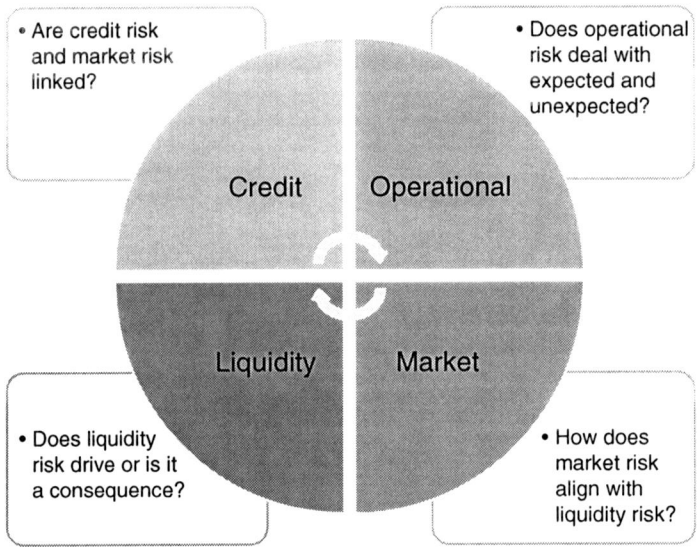

In the graphic, I have suggested four risks, but they are clearly not mutually exclusive and may not be suitable for your firm. The risks that you will model will come from the risk identification process we have discussed and the concentrations that you have identified as sensible to appropriately capture the risks.

In this case, the risks are all associated with each other, so there must be some form of correlation operating. What that means is that while the risks do not operate in isolation, they probably will not all occur at the same time. If we say that the risk appetite is $100 million, we could do something as follows:

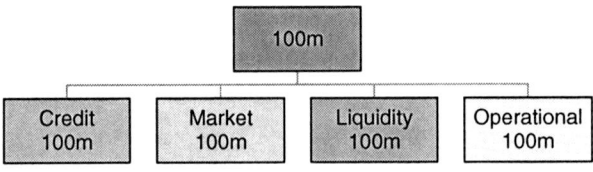

However, this assumes that every risk could occur in isolation only, which is really not realistic. If you think about the impact of a large credit loss, it would affect the market risk and if there is a collapse in the market, that clearly impacts liquidity. What needs to be done is to look at what actually happened during events that have occurred in the past and what the consequences of this were.

If we put $25 million in each of the four boxes, then the modelling would assume that all the risks would take place at the same time. Clearly that can also not always be the case. Just because your inventory has been destroyed, it does not mean you will necessarily have a major increase in credit risk. So, that will also be probably wrong. It will also mean that the first level of the cascade of risk management totals the original risk appetite. That essentially will result in your overcontrolling the business and will result in a suboptimal outcome. So, the answer will follow undertaking real analysis which, with regret, is not easy. The outcome would be something looking a bit like this:

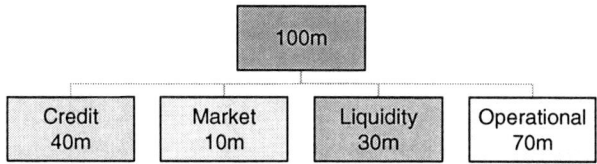

In this case, the first level of the risk appetite cascade totals $150 million, so there is a clear correlation benefit from undertaking the analysis. You now have a series of figures that cannot exceed the original risk appetite values of $100 million, but now will tell you the figure you need to use to build the remainder of the risk management structure. Basically, you would now design an operational risk management framework that ensures that the total loss from operational risk will not exceed $70 million.

This means that the individual risk appetite will need to be cascaded down to the level at which the control has a clear owner and consequently is actively managed. Throughout the analysis, you are undertaking an analysis of correlation between risks and then cascading down to the level at which the risk is being controlled. This sounds like complex mathematics, but so long as you keep your objectives clear, you will understand what you need to do. Perhaps equally importantly and will also understand what you do not need to do.

In this case, you are looking for information that tells you something about the nature of the risks that you are seeking to control. You are looking for data stability that will make the data reliable within the modelling you want to conduct. However, nothing that you can do will be particularly accurate, so much of your data will only be supportive of what might be termed as "on average assumptions". What this means is that they will assist you with understanding what you expect to occur. Modelling which is designed to identify remote or unlikely events will be even less accurate, but should provide you with some form of insight into events that could happen, but have not happened to date.

The modelling of risk appetite down to the level at which the risk is controlled is still an emerging science. It is probably easiest to understand this in a graphic as follows:

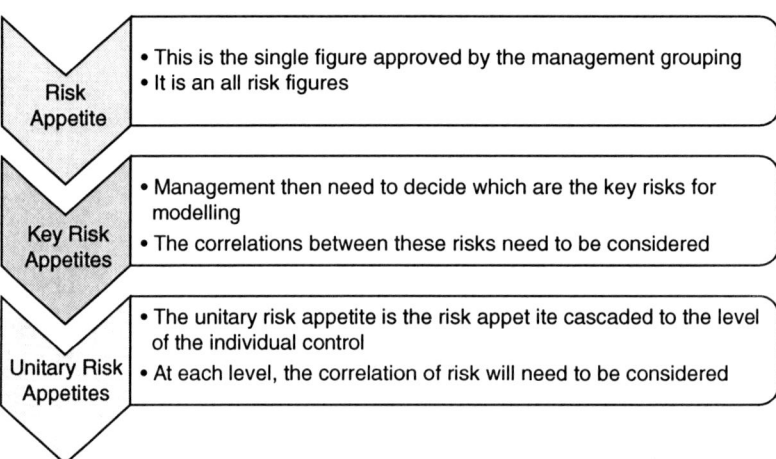

What you need to do is to conduct sufficient analysis at each level of the cascade and then consider what correlation is likely to occur. If at a new level of the cascade you think that it is likely that all of the areas of risk you are looking at could occur together, then you will conclude that there is a high level of correlation. If this is not the case, then there will be a low level of correlation.

You then need to cascade the risk appetite down to the level at which it is being controlled so that the control applying can be designed to ensure that the unitary risk appetite is not breached. This risk appetite modelling then shows how the individual control contributes to ensuring that the entire business is controlled in accordance with risk appetite.

What this means in practice is that as the risk appetite of the firm changes, senior management then have the opportunity to consider whether any of the unitary risk appetites should also raise. However, a clear warning here—Do not get lost in the mathematics! Keep a clear idea of what you are trying to achieve and make the best estimates you can using mathematical techniques where these are likely to add value.

If the risk management modeling professionals make everything too complex, they run the risk that your senior management may not understand what you are trying to achieve and that could become career-limiting.

Remember that the objective is to provide senior management with a better understanding of the nature of their control environment and to provide them with the levers to enable them to manage them. Risk is the real currency of the business. When risk appetite is managed effectively it can be used to ensure that everything within the business is managed consistently with the objectives of achieving a common goal.

If your management is able to understand and articulate complex mathematics, go ahead and then use them—otherwise avoid them as much as possible.

Risk appetite modelling is perhaps the most important building block within risk management and it is well worth spending time on this area to ensure that it is adding value and well understood.

CHAPTER 8

Risk Register

The risk appetite modelling is the most important element of any risk management framework, regardless of industry or location since it enables management to articulate their control environment. As they are willing to take more risk, they can increase the risk appetite. If they wish to take less risk, they will reduce their risk appetite.

However, to be able to do this in any consistent basis will require the development of a consistent risk register. While this is easy to state, in practice, it has been hard to implement. In this chapter, we will look at why this has been a problem and the solutions.

What Is a Risk Register?

A risk register is certainly not a regulatory construct. Rather, it is one of the key tools used to ensure that risk management is embedded within the organization. To meet its objectives the register needs to include all the risks that are faced by the firm in a language that is common to all its users. A register needs to be embedded and used as well as owned by every business unit management and not by some mythical risk department.

While it is easy to say that all risks must be included, this is not easy to achieve in practice. There are some risks that will be common to all business units within a firm and others will be specific to a single business unit. The management grouping needs to think through the common elements of risk that which will apply to all business units. These will be items such as:

- The risk of internal fraud
- The risk of customers failing to meet contractual obligations

- The risk of running out of money
- The risk of losing key skills

The first risk is typically one of the risks included within operational risk. However, the term *operational risk* is rarely well understood and is too frequently confused with *operations risk*, more of which later.

The second risk is clearly a credit risk, but one of a series of credit risks that a firm needs to consider.

The third risk is essentially liquidity risk and it is often due to problems with liquidity risk that firms most frequently fail. This can occur when a firm is growing or recovering as well as when it is failing.

The final risk initially might be thought to be part of each risk, but is not. Loss of key skills may cause many other risks to increase, but that is a consequence, not a cause. Operational risk normally is defined as covering people, process, systems and external risk. As such, this risk is included within operational risk.

By using specific language that is likely to resonate with the audience that is using the information and avoiding generalizations, the risk appears to be relevant to the user. If it is obviously relevant, then the management of a specific business unit may be willing to assist with establishing the extent of the risk. However, for the governance grouping, it will be important to bring all of this together through the medium of risk appetite, so a mapping to a small number of risk is still required. This list is often as follows:

- Credit risk
- Liquidity risk
- Operational risk
- Market risk
- Reputational risk
- Strategic risk

The management team will work together on deciding on the risks that will be common to all business areas and will agree these definitions. When developing the definitions, they should ensure that the language they use is appropriate for the audience for which it is intended. Too often, quality risk programs fail due to lack of implementation within the business, and appropriate use of language is crucial in achieving this.

Developing the Risk Register

At this stage, all you have developed is a list of key risks developed by the management grouping. This needs to articulate both internal and external risks—that is, the risks that the business is able to manage and those that it cannot. Failure to recognize risks that a business cannot manage can often be a cause of failure as the firm has failed to plan to manage a risk that is outside of their sphere of control, such as government action, for example.

The next stage is to complete the list of risks that the firm is subject to. As mentioned, some of these will be within the control perjure of the firm itself whereas others will not. Some will be general to all business units and others will be specific to a single business unit. This is where the workshops come in.

Firms are often too ambitious in their objectives for risk workshops, and from experience you should separate work on risk identification from work conducted on quantification and control. By separating the tasks into something that is manageable, you are able to work with unitary management using a language that means something to them.

Developing the Unitary Risk Appetite

The workshop conducted with the business unit will need to look at the general risks that have been identified by the senior management grouping and then start to consider what this really means to the business unit. Sometimes, the general risk will essentially be redefined into the language of the business unit. In other cases, new risks will be identified, which are more relevant to the business unit management and these will also need to be mapped to the general risks identified by the management grouping.

Local management will not have any real understanding of risk. As we discuss in the next chapter, they have not normally been properly trained to think about risk. Now they are being encouraged to do so. This means that the workshop that is to be used to identify the unitary risks needs to be properly planned and deal effectively with the limited risk understanding of the audience. They know what they are controlling, not what they should be controlling.

The first issue is who should run the workshop. The role of the facilitator is crucial since the success of the workshop will hinge on the ability of the facilitator to engage with the unit management and tease out the risks that they either do or do not control. Before the facilitator commences the workshop, they will need to do a lot of planning.

This will include looking at the things that have gone wrong in the unit to learn which risks they face and do not currently adequately control. They will need to understand the nature of the activity conducted and look at the way that risks are currently controlled.

The next task is to think through the totality of the risks faced by the business unit, regardless of whether or not they are controlled. Workshops frequently fail through focusing on the risks that the business currently controls, rather than those that it fails to recognize at all.

Structure of the Risk Register

There are some elements that are common to all risk registers. These are as follows:

1. The name of the risk
2. The description of the risk in a language that unitary management will understand
3. The owner of the risk
4. How the risk is managed and controlled
5. How the risk is measured

The risk owner should be the person who has responsibility for the risk. They should have the ability to manage the risk and receive sufficient reliable reporting to enable them to know when problems are likely to occur.

How the risk is currently controlled and managed should be recorded in the register. This should be a statement of what is currently achieved, not a view about what might potentially be achieved in the future. The risk register is a live document used by management on a regular basis, not something that is imposed upon them and is theoretical.

The real problem comes with measurement, as we shall discuss in more detail later. Some risks have agreed methodologies for measurement and these should clearly be used. However, some risks are not easy to measure with any degree of accuracy. How would you measure the risk of government intervention or a terrorist event? Of course, not everything can be measured accurately.

Unless the risks are measured, how could you track the effectiveness of your control strategy? Measurement will probably involve a combination of judgment and measurement, but some form of numeric format for judgment is still required.

There are some real challenges here, not the least of which is dealing with both relevance and scaling, but more of this later.

CHAPTER 9

The Three Lines of Defense Model

The three lines of defense model should be used by all firms as a basis for structuring their risk and control process. At its most basic, it appears as follows:

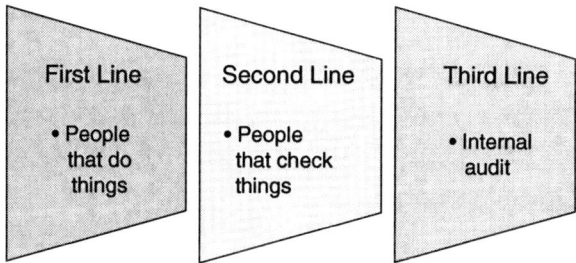

The first line of defense includes anyone that creates transactions, that operates the business that sells or records things. Each of these business units will have a risk register and they will record in those registers the controls that they employ to prevent manifest error or other problems.

The second line of defense includes internal control and consists of is those units that check things as a function. Areas such as compliance and risk management are also part of the second line of defense since they do not initiate transactions. However, front line supervision is part of the control structure applied by those that are responsible for entering into transactions and therefore this is often considered as part of the first line of defense.

You need to remember that each unit within the second line of defense will also have a risk register. They still need to effectively manage their responsibilities and have their risks aligned to the work that they conduct. These will include internal and external fraud, misreporting and loss of key skills, for example.

As the risk management structure of your business is refined, you may start to wonder who is responsible for the second line of defense. Surely, someone should be appointed with overall responsibility for this important area.

Finally, we have the third line of defense—internal audit. Their job is to undertake a periodic review of business areas in accordance with the instruction of the audit committee. As such, they are part of the control structure, but independent of it.

By applying the three lines of defense model, a firm is able to implement sufficient checks and balances to ensure that the business is managed and controlled in the way that the governing management want. Of course, there are always problems with any structure, but good people can make any structure work.

The key issue for the first line of defense is to not seek to actively rely upon the second line of defense to prevent losses occurring. Often, the second line is in a position whereby they can record a loss that has occurred, but there is nothing they can do to prevent its occurrence. They are often a detective lagging control, rather than a loss preventing leading control. As a business puts in more and more controls, the consequence of this could be that the first line of defense may become lax and increasingly error prone, seeking to rely on the second line of defense.

Remember, controls are for bad people. If nobody did anything wrong, we would never need controls. However, we have businesses where errors and mistakes are made and clearly the controls are necessary to try to prevent the loss. These leading controls are the ones that really add value. Lagging controls which result in detecting and recording losses are as useful as counting the dead on the battlefield, not winning the war.

The next problem can be the second line of defense itself. They have a habit of starting to do things themselves that they think are not currently being done properly. This is never the right answer. In all cases, they need to ensure that they facilitate the first line of defense, taking control for their own actions.

Finally, there is internal audit trying to be independent although they are still employees of the firm. They have a key problem in being seen to add value while potentially also being seen as the spies in the camp. Internal audit can also fall into the trap of doing things that should have been done by either the first line of defense or the second line of defense. As mentioned before, they also have concerns about what might best be termed as career-limiting audit findings. Big findings often involve some level of criticism of senior management, sometimes very senior management. Making findings in this area is always high risk for an internal auditor. However, it is part of their responsibility to ensure that this is undertaken diligently but with the greatest of care.

From our experience, some audit functions fail to address some of these key areas, to the detriment of the control framework being applied.

CHAPTER 10

Risk Training

As we move into the more detailed areas of risk management, it is only right to spend a few minutes considering risk training. Risk management involves everyone from the chairman to the doorman. It includes considering outsourced service providers and contractors as much as employees.

Few staff are actually hired due to their knowledge of risk management and indeed many do not need believe that they need either risk management skills or mathematical skills to undertake their daily work. They are being hired to do a task, often with limited latitude for innovation or variance.

If you are seeking to implement a risk management framework, you will need to involve all the staff in the process. They need to understand their role in the framework and what it means for the job they do on a day-to-day basis.

They will be asked to think about things that might go wrong, as opposed to just being beaten up about things that have gone wrong in the past. This work could be conducted by the same staff who have previously been criticized whenever something is found to be wrong—and you now want them to admit things that have not even happened yet. Even worse, you expect them to be able to evaluate the impact of the uncertain event. Basically, they are unlikely to be able to do this without a significant investment in structured training.

There are accredited risk qualifications available, but these are unsuitable for most staff. Instead, the firm needs to develop its own training program that fits the market in which they operate. It needs to be commensurate with the size and complexity of the firm.

The key model that tends to be adopted looks at the following:

$$\text{Severity} = \text{Event x Probability}$$

If you are intending to ask staff about probabilities of things occurring, then they will need to understand basic mathematical techniques. Do not underestimate your challenge here.

Many people in management, even senior management, have very limited understanding of mathematical techniques. For lower level staff, expectations rather than knowledge levels could be even lower. Clearly, some degree of mathematics training is likely to be useful. Businesses use such business mathematics all of the time, yet the skills frequently are not there to enable the techniques that are available to be used and communicated effectively.

All staff need to understand the point of having a risk management framework. They also need to understand the difference between severity, as defined above, and the actual loss that is being considered. Remember, in any case where an event loss exceeds the unitary risk appetite, it must not be allowed to occur. It is not the severity that is taken against the risk appetite, it is the actual value. It is that loss that is unacceptable, not a percentage of it.

This training needs to be practical and relevant, focusing on the things that matter most to the audience. The values of the program need to be emphasized without making the whole process appear as a regulatory construct. If employees are provided with sufficient training so that they can understand their role in this process, then they just might reduce the level of errors that they make and get things right.

The issue of outsourced suppliers and contractors is also important. Just as new starters receive an induction program, including risk management, likewise consideration should be given to extending this to outsourced suppliers and third parties.

Finally, do not forget the Board and particularly non-executive directors. Since they are going to be provided with information on risk management, they had better be able to understand it.

In terms of how long the training should be, this will depend on the structure that you adopt. Many firms choose to appoint risk champions within individual business units who will have a higher level of training and knowledge than that provided to all staff.

If that is the structure applied, then the following depth of training may appear to be appropriate:

Role	Length of Training
Board	Half day
Non-executive directors	Half day
Senior management	One day
Risk champions	Three days
All staff	Half day

CHAPTER 11

Risk Metrics

Without having the ability to effectively measure risk, it will not be possible for the management team to properly assess whether their risk management strategy is either appropriate or cost-effective.

Risk metrics enable management to appreciate the extent to which risk is being effectively managed within the organization and if there are arising risks that need to be considered. To build an effective risk management framework, it is important to commence by working on establishing data availability and accuracy. Without adequate data, the company will be guessing what the position might be and this may or may not be reliable.

Risk metrics fall into a series of classes, including the following:

- Metrics that enable management to understand the risk they are taking
- Metrics that enable management to understand the risk they are mitigating
- Leading indicators, that provide information on a problem the company may be facing, to enable corrective action to be taken
- Lagging indicators, that provide information on problems that the company has already faced so corrective action can be taken.
- Key risk indicators, which are weighted metrics of risk that provide management with a key snapshot of what is occurring.

There needs to be a clear understanding of the level of risk currently being taken by the company. It works from the initial assessment of the risks that are included in the risk register. Remember that these risks will include those that the company can control and those that it cannot (for example, external risks such as taxation changes). Just because a company cannot control a risk does not mean it will go away just as floods and earthquakes will not go away.

The level of risk being suffered by the firm—termed inherent risk—can be thought of as being the level of loss that would be incurred if there were no controls being maintained. A business needs this information to enable them to understand whether the control structure that they are employing is cost-effective and adding value. Too often, as we shall see, this is not the case.

Information on risk here should be aligned to risk appetite as previously discussed, highlighting the chance that the goals and missions of the firm are unlikely to be achieved. It also needs to be provided to management in a format using graphical presentation to enable them to synthesize the key information. Too often, the risk management team produce information in a manner which senior management are either unable to understand or completely misunderstand.

We would generally expect such reporting to be in pure value terms. As we shall see, even qualitative data can easily be put into value terms and shown graphically.

However, the risk team need to understand that apart from the actual level of risk being encountered as a consequence of the activity being undertaken, it is the direction of travel that is particularly important for management.

Will there be a metric provided to the Board on every risk and what really is inherent risk? Answering the first question, the Board or governing grouping will be interested in any risk where there is a risk appetite that needs to be monitored.

If a risk appears to be inconsequential they would not expect to have it reported to them other than perhaps annually to confirm that it is indeed inconsequential. However, there is always the chance that the inherent risk assessment itself may be incorrect or matters that ought to have been considered have not been properly considered.

This can mean, for example, that a company might think they have no risk of a flood since they have never had a flood. The failure to appreciate the risk will mean that any potential mitigation that could have been considered will, in effect, be ignored.

In terms of the inherent risk assessment, there is a real problem. If you ask someone to come up with a value for inherent risk for internal fraud, for example, how would it be calculated? Residual risk as shown in the internal loss data as considered later is only a subset of inherent risk. Often the control environment mitigating the inherent risk will have been fully effective and no loss would be incurred.

So residual risk is not very effective in enabling you to calculate or even estimate inherent risk. However, remember that inherent risk must be at least as large as residual risk.

Another issue is that if a large loss has occurred and management have stated that this is a one-off, they could be doing the business a disservice if they implement a suitable control. An event that is unlikely will occur from time to time, but the implementation of a control that applies all the time will result in a recurrent loss (the cost of the control) which will be hoped to mitigate the event were it to recur (which it might never do).

But inherent risk just like residual risk is a distribution; it is not a single value. The value that you really want to get to is the area under the curve. Different types of event can occur and have different impacts, with each occurring with a different probability. An event that has a 1 percent likelihood may have an inherent risk much lower than an event with a 10 percent likelihood.

If you ask someone to give you a value for an inherent risk, what data will they provide? What will they be thinking? Expected potential loss?

Maximum potential loss? The largest loss they can imagine? Somewhere in-between? In the absence of training and the provision of appropriate examples it is unlikely that management will be in a position to provide the required information reliably or consistently.

The other issue we need to consider is key risk indicators. It is unrealistic for a single metric to be a key risk indicator and as mentioned they are generally weighted metrics made up of a series of leading indicators. These metrics need to be back tested. That will involve looking at events that have occurred in the past and seeing if these metrics would have identified them before they occur.

Key risk indicators need to be predictive otherwise, what is the point? A key risk indicator is not needed to tell you that you have a loss. Accounting does that perfectly well. KRIs look at a range of factors, both internal and external, and synthesize them into a model which hopefully will tell you when risk is increasing. The objective is to take early risk mitigative action rather than just waiting until a loss occurs.

CHAPTER 12

Internal Loss Data

What is the point of internal loss data? It is so hard to get and it is so hard to use.

When considering enterprise risk management, internal loss data does have a role; but perhaps it is not as sophisticated as some might think. Basically, internal loss data can tell you quite a lot about what has previously gone wrong, but it is rarely complete or accurate. The logic is that, in part, it will tell you about the losses that you generally incur and assist you with working out what budgeted losses should be. But how useful is it? Let's explore that further.

Internal losses are the losses that arise because of your choice of internal control system. Generally, the weaker your control system, then the higher the level of losses that you will probably incur. But you need to be careful here. If, on average, you lose $25,000 a year from an event or style of loss and to prevent it would cost $50,000, then you would take the $25,000 loss every time. But are losses really like that? Do they work on average?

There are the losses that you expect to take place all the time and others which occur less frequently. Controls are often designed to either prevent or identify losses that are normal, but they are often weak at identifying less usual losses; such as those arising as a result of fraud.

It is unrealistic to expect a control designed to prevent problems in the day-to-day to be effective when you are considering extreme values.

Risk management need to therefore consider what internal loss data is and what it is for. There are two types of internal loss data:

1. The losses that result from events that you expected to happen; and
2. The losses that result from events that you did not expect to happen

Considering first losses that you did expect to happen, these fall into many categories. As already discussed, risk management is not about budgeting and loss distributions are curves showing loss severity and likelihood over the extent of a distribution.

You might expect five losses from a particular type of event over a year, but you might not expect 50. You might expect an individual loss of up to $120,000, but not a loss of $4 million. As you can see, an expected loss might be unexpected due to either value or frequency. It could be expected by nature, but unexpected by consequence, or it could be unexpected by frequency.

Unexpected losses are really the manifestation of some form of scenario and we will consider this in depth later. Generally, any loss that is incurred that is a manifestation of a scenario is not relevant for internal loss data modelling. It is the occurrence of an unlikely event. This does not make the event necessarily more likely tomorrow or tell you that much about the nature of the next event that might occur. If such events are in the database, take them out.

For internal loss data to be useful, it needs to be aligned to the nature of the business that you intend to conduct. The key value of internal loss data is in assisting management in assessing the quality of their control environment and how it contributes to the achievement of the goals and missions of the firm. As such, it needs to be related to the business that you are intending to conduct.

That means that any loss that took place a few years ago needs to be considered to ensure that it remains relevant, but the value also needs to be fully considered. A loss from 3 years ago, were it to occur today, could occur at a different value. Perhaps the average value of the transactions that you conduct has changed. Perhaps the loss is no longer relevant.

Taking the scaling issue first, to make internal loss data effective, it is necessary for the risk management professionals to consider what the loss would be were an equally significant loss to occur now or in the future. This, by its nature, may have a different value. The consequence of this is that an internal loss database is not static and all losses included within it need to be regularly reassessed to ensure that the values remain valid.

However, the loss itself might not be relevant. If you are ceasing a certain product or service, then clearly, the losses related to that product or service will cease to be relevant and should be excluded from any future analysis.

Similarly, if you are replacing a computer system or control structure due to its ineffectiveness, then the losses that relate to the discontinued system will also no longer be relevant. However, the loss database will need to consider the profile of losses that could arise from the new system and that will be undertaken by considering a scenario.

Now you have your database of losses that have been incurred, but how should you assess which value to include? Realistically, most firms do not have effective and fully implemented activity-based costing. What this means is that some areas are considered as cost centers and the costs that they incur are not fully allocated to income streams.

Basically, the internal losses should be fully costed and include both direct and indirect costs. The direct costs are those that directly relate to the event that has caused the loss. This could be the income that is written off or the external consultants that need to be hired to solve matters—for example, lawyers. Then there are the other costs that need to be considered such as supervision, reporting and monitoring.

These costs may well be expensed within other units and would have been incurred, whether the event took place or not. You do need to recognize that the event uses up management and other resources and therefore, these also need to be considered. Internal audit and legal departments are not free and if they are working on non-goal correlated events, then they will not be able to do their job effectively.

So ideally, losses should be fully costed and include both direct and indirect costs. They should be regularly assessed to see that they remain relevant, both in terms of their nature and their value. Also, internal losses as appearing within an internal loss database need to be regularly reported. As you can see they can be a bit of a pain and you do not want a load of them due to the level of modelling that is required.

In terms of their use, you need to look toward the development of a loss distribution. This is done by grouping the losses into value bands, for example:

Value band	Errors identified
0–0,000	
10,001–25,000	
25,001–50,000	
50,001–75,000	
75,001–100,000	
Greater than 100,000	

Each loss that occurs will then be placed into its column and a shape of a distribution will then be developed. This will have a tail to the distribution, but this can be truncated if required. If you do not collect small losses, be very careful.

Just because you do not collect them does not mean they do not exist and have not been already considered in provisioning.

As an example, most managers would not be surprised if they went to one of their staff's houses and found a pencil belonging to the company. That might be considered as pilferage and acceptable to the firm, but it is still a loss. If they went there and found a painting and some tables belonging to the company, then this would be considered as both fraud and a loss, yet both are really losses and both should be considered.

Most firms already own software to turn such a columnar distribution into a curve on which calculations can be conducted. Again, be careful with the tails to the distribution. If you do not collect small losses, it does not mean that they do not exist or are not included within budgets or provisions. Likewise, if losses are included within scenario modelling or stress testing, then these should also be excluded. The loss value from the stress testing or scenario modelling will then be used to estimate the shape of the other end of the distribution.

Be careful when you are using curve fitting software for modelling purposes. Some software has only limited curves available and the curve selected may underestimate median or mode values and also distort tail liabilities. This could undermine what you are seeking to achieve. Some software automatically selects the best fitting curve for you from the ones that are available. Such a selection might fit the expected part of the curve really well but could fail to have the right shape for either of the tails of the distribution. You do need to know what it is that your software is trying to do.

So, what then is the real point of all this work? Clearly, when a loss event occurs, the firm needs to see if they can learn from the event to prevent its recurrence. However, as we shall see, the true value is in confirming the consequence of your control environment and that is where risk and control self-assessment comes in.

These loss investigations should not be a witch hunt. There are many objectives to the work of investigation being conducted, but avoiding the blame culture is important. If staff know that they will be heavily criticized for an event, then they will naturally attempt to suppress knowledge of the event, which is contrarian to the implementation of a successful risk management framework.

The analysis conducted needs to consider whether the event was foreseeable and a consequence of the control environment or whether it was totally unexpected. If a control has been designed to prevent one type of thing happening, then a different event occurring which was not envisaged in designing the control cannot really a measure of the success of the control.

For example, a firm might have a sprinkler system designed to put out a fire within a business unit. If a fire was to occur, then the fire system operating and the loss resulting is expected. That is why the fire system had been installed. However, if there is a failure of an electronic panel causing the fire system to become operational when there was no fire, then this might be termed an unexpected loss. It is a secondary loss and a consequence of your control environment.

If there is a gas explosion, the fire deterrence system will not be effective. You still have the loss, but this is an unexpected loss and should not be compared to the control. The deterrence system was not designed to prevent a gas explosion, so of course, it would not be effective were this to occur.

Indeed, would any control be effective in such a case? You might consider business continuity planning, but this is predicated on staff being available to implement the plan. Mostly, such losses need to be accepted and that is why firms have loss acceptance policies for such losses which they need to keep a watch on and just accept.

Once again, you will be judging the quality and consequences of the control in terms of Value at Risk compared against unitary risk appetite, that is the risk appetite when seen at the level of the control. The loss to be compared will need to be assessed over a suitable period. Normally, 1 year is selected and that is generally consistent with regulatory expectations.

The next challenge is to select a suitable confidence level. As soon as such a confidence level is selected, you run the risk that a loss will be experienced, which is above that confidence level. For this purpose, the selection of 99.9 percent confidence level, which is also known as the soundness standard, will generally ensure that everything is captured with the exception of matters that are the consequence of a really remote scenario occurring, one of those rare events of which we are so concerned.

One way of looking at this loss figure is to consider it as the area under a loss distribution. That means, you look at all the losses that might occur and identify the relevant probability of that type of loss occurring, adding it to the database and including it in the loss distribution. This is then fitted to a curve on which the calculation is taken with the Value at Risk being 99.9 percent of the area under the curve. For more information on this, please refer to the Mathematics of Banking and Finance, which is also published by Wiley Finance.

CHAPTER 13

Risk and Control Self-Assessment

The objectives of risk and control self-assessment are clear. It is management that best understands the nature of their control environment, so it should be management that regularly assesses this as part of their normal controls.

All risk and control self-assessment (RCSA) achieves is to codify this into a consistent format to enable successful reporting to management.

Of course, this does change the role of internal audit and internal control and we shall consider that later.

RCSA starts with the risk register which, as previously discussed, is the articulation of the complete control environment for the firm. Each risk has a clear and concise definition that is understandable by the people that are required to monitor and comply with it. The next challenge is to assess the level of risk that which exists within the business.

This is achieved through asking each of the business units for their inherent risk, which is the level of risk that exists within the business unit in the absence of controls. It should be an assessment of the losses that are likely to occur if the controls were removed, not a figure suggesting that everything will go wrong. In the absence of any controls, not all transactions will be incorrect, it is just that errors that are normally made will neither be identified nor corrected.

There is a problem here. Inherent risk is an estimate, and as such, may well be incorrect. Indeed, the absence of real data almost ensures that it will be unreliable. However, the best people to assess the level of risk must be those closest to the control and issue and that is the local management.

These risks are then matched to the controls that are currently mitigating the risk. Clearly, the impact of the controls is to reduce the likelihood of losses to an acceptable level, which needs to be below the unitary risk appetite. The difference between the inherent risk and the residual risk, that is the risk that remains with your control environment, is the value of your control environment and should be compared to the cost of the control environment.

The residual risk can be compared to actual losses that have occurred to see that they are sensible and of course, inherent risk must be greater than residual risk.

There are a lot of challenges here. Management do not think in terms of risk and have very little understanding of inherent risk. If I ask you, "What level of internal fraud do you expect within your department in the next year?" how would you answer? You might answer that you do not expect any at all. However, is that realistic? Would there be any chance of a fraud, and how would you know? If you knew, you would have stopped it anyway.

Because of this, the initial RCSA analysis is typically based on a facilitated workshop conducted by the risk department. They attempt to tease from the management information which can be used to populate the analysis. Even when I do manage to get a value from you for potential level of fraud in a year, I then tend to ask you for the likelihood, yet how would you know that and would the probability relate to the risk event, such as internal fraud? This is never easy and rarely accurate. Of course, if the controls do massively reduce inherent risk to residual risk, then the controls had better be effective. That means you do require a control indicator to tell you that the controls are operating.

The point of RCSA is not just about what might be perceived as unreliable modelling; rather, it is to get the management to actively consider whether the controls that they are operating are effective and efficient. If they can improve on the effectiveness of your control environment, then this will directly improve upon your bottom line. The actions taken to improve your systems and controls are generally referred to as treatments and their impact needs to be tracked.

So far, I have considered what might be termed as operational risks; however, all risks should be considered, not just those that arise because of the processes you conduct. Consequently credit risk, market risks, liquidity risks, reputational risk and strategic risks should be included, whether they are created by you or imposed upon you.

If, for example, you are involved with an industry that has encountered a high level of government interest, then they could take actions that seriously curtail your business. One example of this might be fizzy drink manufacturers where there is increasing concern at the level of sugar in the drinks. The risk is that government might undermine your activities through either taxation or regulation. The risk mitigating options would include developing lower sugar drinks and also lobbying government. Of course, nothing is without risk and a level of risk still remains.

In terms of credit risk mitigation, this will include obtaining the financial records and ratings related to the firm you are supplying and trying to identify their likelihood of defaulting, that is to say, failing to pay you the sums you are due. To also ensure that you are paid, you have clear contractual arrangements with your customers, setting out clearly their responsibilities. All of this needs to be included within the RCSA.

I mentioned that the roles of internal audit and internal control are now changed. Considering internal control first, part of the second line of defense, they have the responsibility of ensuring that the appropriate level of monitoring is conducted over the first line of defense, including management and supervision.

Now we have the management assessing the level of risk, they will also be looking to the role of internal control in mitigating risks within the business. This begins to look like the first line of defense having oversight over the second line of defense, which would clearly not be sensible. Accordingly, we would suggest that the role played by internal control in mitigating risk should be assessed by internal control as part of the workshop.

The workshop and its facilitation are therefore crucial. The risk professional that works on the initial workshop needs to have a detailed and thorough understanding of the nature of the activity that is being reviewed. This all goes wrong if they do not have that knowledge and therefore, are unable to extract the information from either management or internal control that they require.

These workshops need to be structured, organized and fully documented. The workshop facilitator needs to be booth a listener and a developer of ideas, but it is not their RCSA; it must be owned by management. In future, it will be management that will be undertaking this assessment without reference to the facilitator, who will then move typically into a reviewer mode.

As mentioned, the role of internal audit also changes. Clearly, internal audit as the third line of defense cannot have responsibility for RCSA any more than they can take responsibility for any other area of activity. Internal audit is allowed to provide their input to a process and the RCSA facilitator will undoubtedly find their internal audit reports of interest in considering and assessing the information provided to them by both management and internal control. Of course, internal audit undertakes a program of work as agreed by the audit committee to which they report as a subcommittee of the Board. Nothing in RCSA makes any change to this as a process. The frequency of the assignment is not changed nor should the frequency of the audit be changed.

As an auditor, internal audit will always seek to audit through the control processes operated by management. That ensures that the audit findings resonate with management and are perceived through the structures that are in place. The consequence of this is that the RCSA will be audited as part of the audit that is undertaken. Indeed, this part of the audit will take place during the planning stage of the audit since it will provide the internal auditors with knowledge that will assist them in their audit planning. It will set out the controls that are of greatest importance and the issues that management are already aware of and where they are taking action.

Internal audit should provide management and internal control with the credit for identifying issues and addressing them. This should be clearly stated in the internal audit report since nothing annoys management more than internal audit taking credit for something that they, quite frankly, did not do. Of course, external audit are even worse in this regard when preparing their often poorly thought through and ill-conceived management letters, many of which, by their nature, could be labelled as dangerous. External audit are rarely trained to fully identify and consider changes to control processes and their impact on profitability, raising only matters that have come to their attention in the course of their work. However, without having the time or resources to fully analyze these matters in the manner that internal audit would, it is perhaps unsurprising that so many of these reports fail to achieve their objectives.

So, internal audit should audit the RCSA as part of their routine audit work on every audit they conduct. They will seek to assess whether the most relevant risks were assessed and whether management have appropriately identified the relevant control and monitoring applied. They will review the inherent risk and probability to ensure that there is an audit trail that supports the calculation and that the policies and procedures are adequate. However, they are unlikely to report on the judgments of management due to the level of uncertainty that exists. Unless the inherent risk or probability are manifestly stupid, this is unlikely to turn up in the audit report.

They will also consider the residual risk and control indicators, ensuring that the residual risk has been appropriately compared to the internal loss database, which includes fully costed losses. Such losses need to include all of the indirect costs relating to the event that has occurred, including management time since that has been spent as a consequence of the event occurring.

There is another problem with RCSA, which we do need reflect on. To be effective, it needs to have the involvement of the senior management of the business unit since they will possess the level of knowledge that is required. The first time the exercise is conducted, this is normally the case. Since, ideally, RCSA is part of management's approach to controlling a business area, they should remain fully engaged with the process, yet this rarely occurs. This is one of the areas within risk management where familiarity breeds contempt and increasingly more junior people become involved as RCSA increasingly is seen as a chore, rather than being of benefit to management. Senior management must seek to ensure that business unit remains fully engaged throughout the process and this may require regularly facilitating appropriate workshops to ensure this is achieved.

The Board also need to play their role. They are the sponsors of the entire process and the reporting from the RCSA will assist them in gaining the level of confidence that they require to establish that they are maintaining an adequate control environment. Accordingly, they should be tracking the performance of the RCSA and asking such questions as they consider appropriate to ensure that this important process is working effectively.

CHAPTER 14

Stress Testing

The last tools I will consider in this short test on risk management are perhaps the most important of all—stress testing and scenario modelling. Too often, management are able to understand the day-to-day, but are either unwilling or unable to consider what might be considered as unlikely or unexpected. The problem is that we are living in a world where the most unlikely outcomes are appearing to be prevalent; you only need to look at recent election results globally to know that is the case. Consider things such as interest rates and the oil price. Did you see that happening?

Stress testing commences with sensitivity analysis, which looks at the unitary movement of a key variable. Often, this variable will be something such as:

- Interest rates
- Exchange rates
- Commodity prices
- Housing prices
- Unemployment
- GDP growth
- Market growth
- Transaction volumes
- System downtime

In each case, you can identify a small movement that is likely to occur. Interest rates could move up or down by 25 basis points. The impact that this has on your business tells you a lot about how the business works in practice, its profitability, capital requirements and liquidity. It assists management with understanding the pressures on product pricing and day-to-day management. That is all very well, but what about when tomorrow does not look like today with a small variation? That is the role of stress testing and scenario management.

Stress testing takes sensitivity analysis and moves this to a plausible extreme. Of course, events could occur throughout distribution ending up with the increasingly unlikely events that we are now considering.

If interest rates defined as interbank borrowing rates are at 1 percent, then a sensitivity might be 1.25 percent or 0.75 percent. Sensitivities operate both upward and downward and both would be assessed, but what is the tress value?

The plausible stress event is generally the point at which the relationships between the factors that underpin the sensitivity break down. Essentially, you are unable to continue to infer the value or actions from the input data. For interest rate increases, what might be considered as plausible? Some firms will take the largest value that has ever occurred and others will do some form of estimation.

If interest rates are at 1 percent, would 3 percent be plausible within the one-year view? Or 5 percent? Or 25 percent? How would you assess this?

Most stress events are the result of some form of event occurring that was unexpected, although perhaps, the term *unlikely* is more appropriate.

If a country defaults, then interest rates tend to fly. When Russia defaulted, interest rates hit 150 percent, albeit only for a short period. So, a default of your country would normally result in a massive increase in interest rates. This historic occurrence provides management with some information on what are the consequences of a default. However, there will be issues as to whether they fully appreciate what is likely to be the consequence and the actions that they can take to protect their firm.

Normally, interest rates rise and fall due to either changes in the market or the wish of politicians to meddle with the economy. My view is that this meddling rarely adds value and often results in unintended outcomes. Clearly, there are a lot of possible interest rates between 1 percent and 150 percent and each has a different probability and impact. Indeed, each is likely to lead to a different type of action that management might need to take. At the extreme stress value of 150 percent, a duvet day might seem like a great idea.

So, management should consider the events that would increase interest rates to 3 percent, 5 percent, 10 percent, 15 percent, 20 percent, 25 percent, and so on until such time as the relationships that underpin the stress event break down.

Thinking through what you would do under these scenarios in advance of them occurring is one of the most important parts of this part of the analysis, since were the event to happen, you rarely have the time to properly plan. Indeed, considering the type of event that might cause such a jump in interest rates so that the event can be foreseen is part of the analysis that needs to be conducted.

Stress testing is, however, a rather simplistic two-dimensional view and analysis of risk. It works best where the movement of the sensitivity is not too extreme and it enables management to assess their available options.

A scenario is different. It does not come from a trend. It just happens. Just as plane crashes, flood and volcanoes are all unexpected, each has a consequence and a series of actions that you should take to mitigate the impact of the event. The problem is that there are so many things that could happen.

There are three main sources for scenario data—management knowledge, internal events and external events. Internal events should be included within your internal loss database and might also be used for back testing stress testing. The stress test would then need to consider an event that was either much larger than anticipated or more frequent than anticipated. Remember that we said earlier that when modelling the internal loss database these unusual data points would be excluded since they may not recur. Now they are useful.

The external loss database will also include also include information on events that were so unusual by nature that they might be considered as scenarios. External loss events have happened to other people. To make the information of benefit you need to know what really caused the event, or the data will not be easy to apply. If the external loss results from a volcano, then the cause of the event is clear—it's a volcano? Other events are less clear and require analysis.

Considering a volcano, will you always model it? If you are sitting in the U.K., this leads to the obvious first question: Do we have a volcano?

If there is no local neighborhood volcano, please do not model it. You will know if you have one since it will be quite obvious.

If you do have a local volcano then the database will tell you what might happen based on what has happened when other volcanoes have erupted. You then need to assess what this is likely to mean for your business. What would you lose? Which customers or suppliers would be impacted? How would your bank fare? What about your staff? Would your business continuity plan really work and if not, what else would do you really need to do?

Clearly, you would not place your key processing units on a volcano, yet a firm has. Nor would you place your head office at the end of a runway to an airport—yet, there are firms there. You could put your office anywhere so why place it in an area of heightened risk? These are often decisions taken without regard to scenario modelling. Often the decision that mitigates the scenario is no more expensive than the one that ignores it!

Going back to the volcano you may still need to consider the impact of volcanoes overseas. We saw the business disruption caused by the Icelandic volcano and you will still wish to model the impacts that might result from an overseas volcano eruption if that is relevant to your business.

One case that will appear in your external loss database will concern a disgruntled systems administrator who is able to place a virus in your systems. This scenario caused a major loss for the firm concerned, but the real value to you is to consider the various attributes of the scenario. The first issue is why was the employee disgruntled? In the specific case, they were expecting a bonus of $50,000 and only received $38,000. Rather than saying thank you for the $38,000, they said, "Where is my $12,000?" and took action.

As you are reading this, you are probably thinking who checks your systems administrators. We know what they are supposed to do, we know their policies and procedures, but who checks what they actually do when they are entering a system they are requested and entitled to access?

The second issue is the bonus. Bonuses going up are a motivator, but as they go down, they are frequently a risk management disaster. Do you apply additional controls over such people? Put these two events together and it bought down the computer systems for a major firm.

If I take another case, this will better illustrate what you need to do. A few years ago, I received a newswire saying that the previous day I had received a newswire unchecked and a day early. They claimed that their editor had been sitting at his desk again and had dropped a sandwich sending out the incorrect message. They even provided an electronic trash can to place it in.

A number of issues arise from this simple case. The first is to think through the likely action that will be taken by the recipient of the email. In reality I went into the pam folder where the email always went and looked for the errant message to see what it was that I was not supposed to see.

Essentially, the method of communication probably resulted in more people being aware of the problem than would have otherwise have been the case. The lessons from this are clear. What are your communication plans when something goes wrong and who checks that they add value to your firm?

The next issue is with the errant message. I tried dropping sandwiches onto my computer, but found it difficult to send a message in error. However, when I threw a baguette at the right key, it was possible.

That falls into the *so unlikely* that it is probably apocryphal and nobody fancies eating apocryphal sandwiches. So, probably just a message that escaped rather than being properly approved and released.

Now, you have a general problem—a message that should not have been sent. Where in your firm would be the worst place from which to release an incorrect piece of information? Finance with the annual accounts? A letter to a client using inappropriate language? A press release that includes a planned but not confirmed event? Each of these events has an impact and a consequence.

Essentially, what you have done is change a specific case from the external loss database into something generic, and then let it hover over your business. It then attaches itself to the area where it has the greatest resonance and this can then be assessed. The value of scenario modelling is in considering the impact and what you might then be able to do since if the event happens, you rarely have time to think. Of course, there are hundreds and hundreds of possible scenarios. Your problem is that you cannot do them all—but that should not stop you starting.

Another case involved Bristol Zoo. Outside Bristol Zoo was a well-preserved car park where a cheerful chap assisted people going to the zoo, providing them with advertising literature, and of course, taking money for parking. He had a nice little office, where he spent his day and he worked every day the zoo was open. One Monday, he was missing. The zoo management called the Council for a new parking attendant, to which they received the reply that the Council had never had a car park at the zoo.

An enterprising stranger identified the opportunity of using the unutilized space as a car park, prepared it and took the funds for more than 20 years without anyone checking. The fact that nobody even knew his name is perhaps even more strange.

You might think such a case is odd, but could you have someone on your payroll that never comes to work and is still being paid? Could you be paying for a service that you never purchased—a register, for example? Could there be someone that is not really being supervised and is not taking holiday, potentially disguising fraud? Until you do the analysis, you really cannot think this through.

The problem with scenario analysis is that it highlights that controls that work in normal environments might actually become a problem under a stress environment, and understanding that is really important. However, reporting this to senior management can also be a problem. They may not understand the implications, and since the analysis is always incomplete, will rarely know what to do with it. My recommendation is to tell them in general rather than specific terms and see how they react.

CHAPTER 15

Liquidity Risk

All companies have liquidity risk. Some firms see it as essentially cashflow management, whereas others see it as purely managing the bank account. Liquidity is right at the heart of the risk management concerns of any business. Companies need funds to pay their bills, to pay for the goods that they will turn into finished goods, to pay their staff and to pay for other costs that they incur. These include capital purchase, taxation and bonuses, as well as other more routine costs.

Liquidity planning looks at the expected outflow and inflows that the company is expecting and tries to assess whether there are gaps that need to be addressed. Typically, the assessment looks a bit like this:

	Inflows	Outflows	Net Position
0–7 days			
8–14 days			
15–21 days			
21–30 Days			
Month 2			
Month 3			
Later			

The problem is getting the data. Of course, the availability of funding to a company depends upon the nature of the facilities that it enjoys. These will form a number of options including utilization of existing undrawn facilities. It is when comparing the net position to the available facilities to identify whether there is sufficient available funding, which is at the heart of such cashflow management.

At its most basic, the calculation is as follows:

Opening bank position:	X
Add cash inflows	X
Deduct cash outflows	(X)
Net position	X
Available undrawn facilities	Y

So long as Y exceeds X, the company does not have any immediate cash flow problems if the modeling is reliable. However, there are difficulties and other uncertainties, which is why cash flow management and the management of liquidity are such a concern.

In financing itself the company will initially use equity capital and reserves together with finance from the founders often in the form of a loan. Later they can take out loan facilities and extended overdraft facilities as well as issuing bonds which are traded debts with an agreed redemption date. They can also keep reserves rather than distributing them to shareholders in the form of dividend. Liquidity risk management needs to look at the likely market in which options need to be assessed and then consider which option has the greatest likelihood of success.

Accounting records maintained by a firm are generally contractual. They show invoices raised and received and their due dates. These are the contractual dates. Taxation has a set date to be paid, as do salaries, credit card bills, suppliers' invoices, rental charges and other amounts.

However, the actual date on which these will be paid may differ significantly from the original due date.

The contractual payment profile may not equate to the behavioral payment profile that actually reflects what happens. Indeed, customers may not pay on time or might pay early. Such delays in receipts (and of course, there may not actually be a final receipt leading to bad debts) can cause a firm major problems. The behavioral analysis considers what has historically happened and uses this to estimate what the likely position is going to be at the end of any period.

Therefore, liquidity risk management is at its best when it is essentially real-time. There is not a lot of point in knowing that you will have sufficient funds at the end of a period if you do not have the funds during the period to make a payment that is due. Consequently, liquidity risk management continually is assessing the accuracy of the assumptions that are made and taking these into account in their liquidity planning process.

In managing liquidity, there are a number of available tools that can be considered. The first of these is effectively managing the business by actively considering which customers you choose to accept and trying to balance your portfolio appropriately. Ideally, this portfolio management approach will take into account the types of customer that the company has and try to build these into a series of pools. Within these pools, the risks should be essentially similar (or homogeneous).

The objective of liquidity risk management is then to try to balance the portfolio such that if one type of client has financial problems, another is in a better position, leaving the overall cash flow expectations unchanged. This form of portfolio risk management manifests itself in target market analysis, with the company seeking out clients that actually offset other client risks that currently exist within its business.

In deciding upon the facilities that the company requires, they will also need to be consider long-term capital planning. That is raising long-term finance through either the issuance of either equities or bonds. There are again cash flow implications of the choices taken. If a company issues equity and sells it in some way, there is no requirement for redemption, but there is an expectation of a payment of a dividend. It is important to note that the dividend could be passed and if this were to occur, no servicing costs or cash flow implications would result.

If a company issues bonds, they will again receive the cash inflow upfront. However, there is now a definite servicing charge, represented by the coupon on the bonds. There is also a redemption profile set out in the prospectus for the sale of the bonds. Some bonds could be cumulative such that if a coupon is missed, they are paid later, but these are relatively rare. Clearly, both the coupon and the redemption would impact upon cash flow, and consequently, liquidity risk.

Such capital planning is generally long-term although many firms issue bonds every month and operate what are essentially revolving facilities.

The capital planning will also need to take account of the expected investment environment and the position of the underwriters. When a company issues bonds or equities, it will hire an investment bank and an underwriter. The underwriter will take the key risk on the transaction in exchange for a fee. Once they have signed the underwriting agreement, the company knows the amount of monies that it will receive. If the transaction actually fails and nobody actually wants the bonds or the equity, then the underwriter ends up with all of the assets and has to sell them on later.

But there is always a *but*. Even though the underwriter has signed a contract and a price has been agreed, if the market conditions are so badly negative that the transaction is likely to fail, the transaction will generally be pulled. That will mean that the company will not receive the inflow of funds that it anticipated and this could result in major problems for the firm.

That is also why firms have a range of other facilities on which they can call. These include the following:

- Loans
- Overdrafts
- Credit cards
- Invoice discounting or factoring
- Leasing

As always, there are additional problems here. All of these forms of finance carry some type of coupon that the company will have to pay. These eat into the undrawn facilities and result in less funds being available. The loans need to be repaid, something that many firms appear to forget. This includes credit card debt, which is used by many small and medium-sized enterprises for short-term funding.

Invoice discounting and factoring are rather different, by nature. They are essentially designed to enable the company to obtain access to funds on sales earlier than would be the case with normal contractual terms. Of course, there is always a fee for such a service and this is normally built into the funds that the company actually receives.

Facilities are clearly great. They enable a company to trade, knowing that they have the strength of a financial institution behind them. The problem is that the company that does not need facilities can get them and the one that is struggling has facilities removed. That is a problem for cash flow management. The assumption that your financial institution will honor a facility is probably a brave assumption. If a company has a problem with one facility, then often it finds that all the other facilities on which it is relying will be either restricted or withdrawn. This can be extremely frustrating and ultimately may cause the failure of the firm. So undrawn facilities are extremely useful, but it is not correct to assume that they will always be available when they are needed just because they have been agreed to.

The next stage is what are referred to as contingency funding arrangements or plans. These are detailed arrangements which are only activated when the company requires them. They are mostly used by major financial institutions and corporates and are required by banking regulations.

As always, there is a problem. Your firm has contracted to provide contingency funding arrangements for a company and received the relevant fee. The customer then gets into difficulty and calls on you to provide the funding agreed within the contingency funding plan. The provider of the facility is then often left in the position of considering whether the company will fail with the funds provided by the contingency funder or without these additional funds. Of course, the receiver to the failed company might take legal action, but that can be addressed later. My problem with contingency funding plans is the lack of evidence that they are actually effective in practice.

Another issue regarding liquidity risk is for companies that have excess funds. They can either invest these funds into assets, which might provide a source of high quality liquid assets, or they could put them into bank accounts. Bank accounts currently pay very low or limited return, what is essentially a discount to real returns, so can be unattractive. Bank accounts are clearly liquid and might be considered as a low-risk, low-return alternative to investing in other assets. Because of this, many firms go seeking return by investing excess liquidity into other types of financial assets that provide a higher return than the bank accounts. Clearly, the higher return, the higher the risk that the company is taking.

Liquidity risk now considers a number of matters. First, there needs to be an efficient two-way price for any asset acquired that underpins the asset value, based upon prices published by active market makers. If a financial asset ceases to be traded, then its value might become uncertain or limited. While illiquid assets including private equity could generate superior returns, these cannot be guaranteed.

Second, liquidity fund management needs to consider the differing economic environments and their impact upon the asset liquidity. Put at its most basic, if a lot of companies are using similar assets as a stock of high-quality liquid assets, then under adverse local conditions, they will all sell them at the same time. This dumping of the assets onto the market causes a collapse in asset value due to the unbalancing of supply and demand. So, it is necessary to not only consider the high quality liquid assets that you are holding, but to consider them against a variety of economic scenarios.

CHAPTER 16

Credit Risk Management

Credit risk is the risk that you are not paid. When you make a sale, you expect to be paid. You have contractual terms, which you expect your customer will comply with. With regret, this is often not the case.

Credit risk is, however, not just about the risk that your customers fail to make payment on due date. It also arises in other parts of your business, as we shall see.

If a customer fails to meet an obligation or a payment on a loan or overdraft is delayed, then this is called being in arrears. Many firms go into arrears for a variety of reasons and often such amounts are eventually repaid with or without interest. At an extreme, there is a default and the amounts may or may not be lost.

To try to reduce the incidence of this, a credit assessment is undertaken of new and existing customers. In undertaking this work, their financial results will be reviewed and their credit rating considered. This might include, for example, taking information form a reputable credit rating agency. If full credit assessment is undertaken, then this will take into consideration the financial economic environment within which the customer operates. It will consider the following:

- The strength of the customer base
- The quality of the management
- The operational strengths of the business
- Its intellectual property
- The quality of its staff
- The history that the company has of financial success
- The market in which the company operates
- Its competitive pressures
- The impact of innovation on the likely success of the firm

Such issues will, of course, need to be considered, depending on the level of risk that the customer poses to the firm.

Credit risk also occurs in other areas. Failure of a major supplier can cause a company significant difficulty. Such suppliers might be providing a product which forms a major part of the company's product offering. However, credit risk also occurs in the case of outsourced service providers. This would include software companies, lawyers and other suppliers. Increasingly, companies outsource more and more. The following is a list of a series of matters that might be outsourced, but of course, it is not likely to be complete.

The following services can be outsourced:

- Marketing
- Payroll
- Internal audit
- Debt recovery
- Legal and compliance
- Accounting
- Processing
- Systems development
- Systems administration
- Security
- Cleaning
- Logistics
- Warehousing

There is no limit to this anymore. Companies increasingly seek to focus on the areas where they add the greatest value and move the remainder to a firm that seeks to focus on delivery of this service as a specialist skill.

However, if the loss of such a supplier would be critical to the success of the company, then this will need to be factored in. Basically, all such firms should be credit assessed to ensure that their failure is properly assessed.

In such cases, the focus will be on the financial position of the firm, but another problem occurs. Smaller firms are generally private and consequently will either not have audited accounts or will have accounts that have been audited by what might be termed as smaller firms. Many such firms are advisors to the company concerned and provide advice on a range of other issues that might be considered to impact upon their objectivity.

In a private company, there is often a dominant individual who could remove all the available funds in the company without recourse to a third party. This position would not exist in a larger firm, which generally requires multiple layers of control. The consequence of this is that it may not be as possible to rely upon the accounts to the extent that the firm might wish to do so. Accordingly, in such cases, the company will often request details of the insurance that the company maintains, in part to mitigate this risk.

There is, in addition, credit insurance which will pay out and is generally based on a change in the rating of a counterparty. This might make sense for a major corporate credit exposure, but the cost would make it prohibitive in other cases.

CHAPTER 17

Putting It All Together

So, we have started with governance and looked through the main approaches a company can adopt to implement enterprise risk management. This is a series of techniques that many firms have been slow to implement.

For the Board, the process needs to commence with the key risks analysis and you then need to see that they buy into this. These risks will change from time to time, although some remain the same. Issues such as:

- The economy
- Interest rates
- Competition
- Government action
- Fraud and criminal activity

will always be there, but others will vary, depending on your firm. For some firms, some or all of the following will need to be considered:

- Exchange rates
- Innovation
- Technology
- Model risk
- Strategic risk
- Pensions
- Quality
- Processing
- Commodities

The list is not quite endless, but there is so much that could be included and it needs to relate to the firm concerned. The next stage is to assess risk appetite, work on the correlations and then cascade it to the level of the control. Now, use RCSA to work out your controls and monitoring, assess the risk and ensure risk appetites are not exceeded. Back test using real internal loss data, then move to stress testing and scenario modelling to try to think through what really matters.

Finally, try to get senior management involved. Design a reporting system that allows you to identify trends in the data that tell your management about how things are changing and helps them to think through what they need to do. They may not understand why they are doing it. They may not be very good at doing it. But when the impossible happens, they will be pleased that they did.

Enterprise risk management is about a vision that needs to be applied in practice. Staff within the business at all levels need to really understand the risks that are inherent in the activity that they are undertaking, that includes all the risks, not just the operational risks. Everyone has the brand in their hands and their failure can make a significant difference.

Recent cases of BP and Volkswagen have bought this into clear focus.

Risks do not occur separately. When something goes wrong, there is often a perfect storm of a combination of all risks at once. Credit, operational, liquidity, strategic and reputational risks can all occur at the same time. Too often, complacent management fail to appreciate the way that risks interact and limit their ability to maneuver the company effectively.

Risk management is not a slogan, it is a way of working—indeed, it is probably the only way a company can operate effectively. Risk management needs to be embedded into everything that the company does, in everything it says and delivers. This goes from peripheral and physical security through cyber security to strategy, credit, liquidity and then to other operational risks.

Through the application of risk appetite and risk acceptance policies, a firm can better understand the nature of the risks that they are taking. Staff appreciate the nature of the risks that they are managing and their role within risk management. As we have said before, you do not need the greatest risk management department and Chief Risk Officer; rather the need is for effective risk management embedded within the business. This is your real challenge.

Index

OTHER TITLES IN OUR FINANCE AND FINANCIAL MANAGEMENT COLLECTION

John A. Doukas, Old Dominion University, *Editor*

- *Money Laundering and Terrorist Financing Activities: A Primer on Avoidance Management for Money Managers* by Milan Frankl and Ayse Ebru Kurcer
- *Introduction to Foreign Exchange Rates, Second Edition* by Thomas J. O'Brien
- *Rays of Research on Real Estate Development* by Jaime Luque
- *Weathering the Storm: The Financial Crisis and the EU Response, Volume I: Background and Origins of the Crisis* by Javier Villar Burke
- *Weathering the Storm: The Financial Crisis and the EU Response, Volume II: The Response to the Crisis* by Javier Villar Burke
- *Rethinking Risk Management: Critically Examining Old Ideas and New Concepts* by Rick Nason
- *Towards a Safer World of Banking: Bank Regulation After the Subprime Crisis* by T.T. Ram Mohan
- *The Penny Share Millionaire: The Ultimate Guide to Trading* by Jacques Magliolo
- *Escape from the Central Bank Trap: How to Escape From the $20 Trillion Monetary Expansion Unharmed* by Daniel Lacalle
- *Applied International Finance Volume I, Second Edition: Managing Foreign Exchange Risk* by Thomas J. O'Brien
- *Tips & Tricks for Excel-Based Financial Modeling, Volume I: A Must for Engineers & Financial Analysts* by M.A. Mian
- *Tips & Tricks for Excel-Based Financial Modeling, Volume II: A Must for Engineers & Financial Analysts* by M.A. Mian
- *The Anti-Bubbles: Opportunities Heading into Lehman Squared and Gold's Perfect Storm* by Diego Parrilla
- *Applied International Finance Volume II, Second Edition: International Cost of Capital and Capital Budgeting* by Thomas J. O'Brien
- *Hypocrisy of the African Public Finance Management Framework: The Case of Malawi* by Kamudoni Nyasulu

Announcing the Business Expert Press Digital Library

Concise e-books business students need for classroom and research

This book can also be purchased in an e-book collection by your library as

- a one-time purchase,
- that is owned forever,
- allows for simultaneous readers,
- has no restrictions on printing, and
- can be downloaded as PDFs from within the library community.

Our digital library collections are a great solution to beat the rising cost of textbooks. E-books can be loaded into their course management systems or onto students' e-book readers. The **Business Expert Press** digital libraries are very affordable, with no obligation to buy in future years. For more information, please visit **www.businessexpertpress.com/librarians**. To set up a trial in the United States, please email **sales@businessexpertpress.com**.

CPSIA information can be obtained
at www.ICGtesting.com
Printed in the USA
FFOW02n0710171117
43596244-42394FF

9 781947 098442